Positive Teaching,
Positive Learning

Positive Teaching, Positive Learning is an ideas book for the classroom with practical suggestions for generating and interpreting positive feedback.

Rob Barnes draws on many years of teaching experience and extensive research to propose six core aspects of positive teaching and learning. These include: learning to understand and re-describe difficulties so that they can be minimised; the ways in which high expectations for classroom feedback can be generated; the use of descriptive praise; and the ways in which both pupils and teachers can avoid unnecessary stress through taking a more realistic yet positive view of their lives. Each of these central ideas defining positive teaching and learning is supported by suggestions for practical strategies which have been used successfully in the classroom.

Teachers, lecturers, educational psychologists and anyone concerned with special needs will find this book useful, inspiring and practical.

Rob Barnes is Senior Lecturer in Education at the University of East Anglia. His previous publications for Routledge include *Teaching Art to Young Children 4–9*, *Art, Design and Topic Work 8–13* and *Successful Study for Degrees*. These and other publications focus on creative thinking applied to teaching and learning.

Positive Teaching, Positive Learning

Rob Barnes

London and New York

First published 1999
by Routledge
11 New Fetter Lane, London EC4P 4EE

Simultaneously published in the USA and Canada
by Routledge
29 West 35th Street, New York, NY 10001

Routledge is an imprint of the Taylor & Francis Group

Typeset in Goudy by Keystroke, Jacaranda Lodge, Wolverhampton
Printed and bound in Great Britain by Creative Print and Design (Wales), Ebbw Vale

British Library Cataloguing in Publication Data
A catalogue record for this book is available from the British Library

Library of Congress Cataloging in Publication Data
Barnes, Rob.
    Positive teaching, positive learning / Rob Barnes.
    Includes bibliographical references and index.
    1. Teaching. 2. Effective teaching. 3. Learning, Psychology of.
    4. Teacher–student relationships. I. Title.
    LB1025.3.B34   1998
    371.102–dc21   98–49944

ISBN 0–415–18139–9

After emerging from a cell measuring 7 ft by 7 ft,
Nelson Mandela, President of South Africa,
described how this had been his home for eighteen years:
'There were pleasant and unpleasant
experiences', he said, 'and it depends on how
you look at the situation.'

Contents

Figures and tables

Figures

Table

Acknowledgements

This book could not have been written without the inspiration of many teachers over the years. In particular, I would like to thank Deborah Berrill, Janet Collier, John Etheridge, Peter Gibley, Miriam Holzer, Andrew Lawes, Bill Rogers, Monica Tester, Cathy Whalen and Annette Willington. I am also grateful to all those trainee-teachers who had the courage to try out many of my ideas without prejudice and tell me what they thought.

Chapter 1

Positive and negative thinking

Sophie was not supposed to improve, and why she did is a question that has resurfaced many times during my teaching career. The mother of this fresh-faced 12-year-old was the librarian at the art school where I was a student. Sophie's mother was adept at finding anything we wanted to know about and seemed always to have book references at her fingertips. She was helpful, knowledgeable and enthusiastic, someone reliable, who could run a generously stocked library where students' questions led her to enthuse rather than frown. Sophie frowned a great deal and would sometimes be there in the evenings when her mother was on the later duty.

When, two years later, I found myself taking over a class in my first teaching post, I was surprised to find Sophie sitting there. Information about pupils was thin on the ground and I assumed she was as bright as her mother. Sophie listened carefully, seemed to enjoy what she was asked to do and wrote pages of steadily improving text. She was involved and she was enthusiastic, just like her mother. Sophie even brought in extra work she had done at home. It was only towards the end of the year that I discovered that she had needed special help in her previous years and had been labelled 'a backward child' by other teachers. Fortunately, the label on this child had gone missing.

According to her mother, Sophie had improved her schoolwork dramatically that year compared with other years. From my point of view, she had done no more than I expected she would, and I was surprised to find she had been any different. The reasons why Sophie improved are no more than informed guesses. Maybe the extra help over previous years had finally paid off. Maybe she just liked the way I taught or she sat next to another pupil who gave her better explanations of the tasks she was to do. I would like to think that she improved because I expected her to, but that is far too simple a reason.

Were my expectations higher than they might have been? There is no shortage of educational advice, counter-advice, research and articles suggesting that high expectations can lead to high achievement and success. A classic example comes from a famous flurry of research activity in the late 1960s and early 1970s, surrounding a controversial experiment by Robert Rosenthal and Lenore Jacobson. Their work is another example of a story that will not go away, and sticks in the mind like Sophie's story of expected improvement. Despite many reservations their critics have voiced about it, Rosenthal and Jacobson's story persists as one of apparent self-fulfilling prophecy. Known as 'Pygmalion in the classroom', their experiment led teachers to think that certain specific pupils would experience an academic growth spurt during the coming year. In reality these children were chosen at random. At the end of the year, 'spurters' demonstrated greater gains in IQ than other children (Rosenthal and Jacobson 1968). In other studies, teachers were told that particular pupils were gifted. Later, their teachers could be observed giving them preferential treatment. Further inquiry looked at naturally occurring teacher expectations and showed that self-fulfilling prophecies can and do occur in the classroom (Seaver 1973). Like the Sophie story, there are reasons why positive effects of this kind are viewed with some suspicion, but they cannot be entirely dismissed.

There are six aspects of positive teaching and learning comprising the main ideas in this book. The first of these is about learning to understand and redescribe difficulties so that they can be minimised. Pupils and teachers can learn practical and optimistic strategies in order to dispute their negative thinking. The second aspect concerns ways in which high expectations for classroom feedback can be created. Do pupils expect that whatever the task there is a strong chance they will need to give feedback? Will feedback be demanded early in a session or project? High expectations include pupil self-assessments, which then inform future teaching and learning. Third, there are ways in which pupils might learn to become responsible, tenacious and self-rewarded through working in a special group exploring their difficulties.

The fourth aspect of positive teaching and learning concerns the use of descriptive praise. There is a powerful, detailed and practical means of giving praise that allows pupils to credit themselves. A fifth aspect is that of developing pupils' positive self-awareness as a result of the feedback they encounter. The sixth aspect deals with ways in which both pupils and teachers can avoid unnecessary stress through taking a more realistic, yet positive view of their lives. There are examples of stress-busting strategies that are known to work for teachers and pupils.

Strategies suggested concern the way we and our pupils can redescribe events to ourselves in more positive ways. If feedback to children about their progress is important – and I believe it is fundamental to their success – it is worth looking at ways to handle negative aspects of this. The strategies are subtle, because there is a fine line between boosting self-esteem and constantly monitoring children so they become dependent on us for approval. Relying on the teacher to approve and say 'That's marvellous, brilliant or wonderful' is not the most positive of responses for children to experience. We do not want to create a situation where pupils depend for the most part on a teacher's approval for their sense of security. An aim of positive teaching is to help pupils to make the best of learning. The role of a teacher is to help them in that process. Improved learning cannot be separated from developing a positive ethos in the classroom. What this means, and how it relates to classroom language and positive comment, are the subjects of the remaining chapters in the book.

A closer look at the Sophie story shows how difficult it is to find reasons. Teachers not only have expectations, but they also remember their pupils' behaviour and achievements in ways that match established beliefs. Way back in the 1970s, Seaver pointed out that a teacher's bias is one of personal perception as well as expectation. Teachers will assign higher grades to pupils they already believe are brighter, and lower grades to those they believe are less capable. In Rosenthal and Jacobson's experiment it could have been that the teachers wanted to describe pupils as having improved whether they actually did or not. There are other effects. Teachers are known to speak differently to pupils depending on how they already perceive them. Studies by Blakey and his colleagues (1971) showed that teachers used a warmer tone of voice when talking with pupils who they believed were high achievers. There are further studies showing teachers treating younger brothers and sisters similarly to the sibling they previously taught. The younger sibling is frequently labelled as a high or low achiever from the outset. There have been other investigations that show how pupils identified as 'gifted' benefit from the teacher's bias. Teachers can also be biased against children they regard as coming from an inferior social and ethnic background (Rist 1970; Babad 1980).

Pupils as positive self-improvers

The idea that high expectations have a positive effect on achievement is ultimately a belief, though one I find attractive. In Sophie's case, my expectations were high and my attitude was positive almost as if by accident. Can positive attitudes be learned? In promoting positive approaches to teaching and learning, I assert six beliefs:

1 Ultimately, negative thinking is wasted energy.
2 Negative thinking feeds on itself.
3 Negative thinking is unnecessarily stressful.
4 Positive optimistic attitudes can be developed.
5 Pupils can take responsibility for becoming positive.
6 Feedback and action are necessary ingredients of improvement.

I also believe that teachers can positively influence pupils' achievement despite the odds. A counter-belief is that pupils' achievement generally matches expectations because teachers are good at forecasting progress. It may not be that they have expectations which influence pupils' achievement, but simply that they forecast their progress so accurately that pupils match that forecast. Nothing unexpected happens. But do children really achieve according to expectations just because the teacher forecasted accurately? Might it be possible for pupils to achieve far more if teachers' expectations were changed for higher ones? The impressive array of research does not conclusively show that expectations bias pupil learning. Nor, significantly, does it show that high expectations have nothing to do with a pupil's success.

If we take the idea that positive teaching includes belief in pupils' almost limitless capacity to improve, there are several consequences. First, the onus is on us to find ways to trigger improvement and to convince pupils they can achieve more than they think. The belief is that if we can only find a way, there will be breakthroughs and rewards for pupils concerning their achievements. This could of course be a recipe for making pupils over-dependent, but it need not be. The onus can be to find strategies that actually include teaching pupils how to learn for themselves. Positive teaching is not just giving pupils a rather generous 'benefit of the doubt' about their difficulties, and plenty of praise, but also about trying to set up the circumstances in which they can be self-improvers. Their rate of improvement and development will vary, but the onus is to teach as if achievement is just around the corner.

We will also need to encourage an attitude that is very high on hope. That hope will be something along the lines that whatever difficulty appears, it is not permanent and pervasive, but specific and temporary and there are ways to change it for the better. An example would be the difference between saying that a pupil cannot spell, and saying that a pupil has not so far remembered the spelling of many words. A high hope factor is different from pretending pupils are achieving when they are not. There is little point in being optimistic about achievement if all that happens is that we lose a sense of reality by distorting perceptions of pupils' results. It would not be very positive to try to hone skills and knowledge beyond children's ability to cope, or ignore their apparent weaknesses.

Positive teaching assumes we will make the most of pupils' potential, building on and describing their successes, rather than defining their limitations. This sounds so familiar that we might easily think we already do it. Faced with the familiar, we can easily fall into the trap of thinking that no self-respecting teacher would do anything but encourage, persuade and be positive towards pupils. How else would we do the job? It is logical to suppose that as professionals we are there to believe in our pupils, take a positive view of their potential and move them forward. It is likely that we may take numerous teaching qualities for granted, such as trying to interest and motivate pupils in what they do, or praising their efforts and achievement. Lidz (1991) summed up the problem of familiarity when describing formative assessment (assessment intended to feed back into learning in order to improve it). She commented that the 'very logic of the idea that formative feedback leads to improvement could lead practitioners to think that they already do it'. Teachers may do all of these things to some extent, but not necessarily create a climate for high hopes of successful learning. Positive teaching is a familiar idea, so familiar that, like believing that people have no reason to drop litter, we might logically expect to live in a litter-free positive world.

The word 'improvement' is a rather flexible one. Believing in pupils' capacity to improve could mean a variety of things, not all of them to do with achievement in a particular subject or skill. Rather in the way we might generalise about the importance of raising standards, 'improvement' suffers from meaning all manner of things depending on how it is used. Desforges (1993: 8) poses two questions about improvement and learners. Can learners do things which they earlier could not do? Can they do things effectively which earlier they did clumsily or slowly? These two criteria are rough and ready reference points, but they at least give a starting point for assessing improvement. It might be that improvement means increased skills or better understanding. Can learners swim faster, for example, or do they understand more clearly why climate changes? It could be that pupils' improvement means that they are better-adjusted human beings whose behaviour helps rather than hinders the smooth running of the classroom. Whatever we define as improvement is likely to mean that pupils have more than they had before, or that the quality of what they achieve is higher.

We need not be over 'picky' about what pupils improve so long as there is a starting point. Improvement can be holistic, so that success in one area of their lives may well spill over into other areas. I confess I have little evidence for this except what I have observed and other teachers have confirmed. I have found that the experience of success can boost self-esteem and give pupils the confidence to learn something new. Starting points for improvement are not quite so hit-and-miss as we might think. Teachers and children choose particular tasks through which to develop learning so these inevitably become the starting points. If children are to improve in their use of computers, for example, they obviously need to be involved in practising tasks using them or nothing much will happen. There is no guarantee that children will improve their skills and understanding, but there is certainly the potential for that. Improvement of the very best kind can be that children believe in themselves where previously they did not.

Feedback, self-esteem and positive comment

There are two main sources of feedback on success and failure when learning anything. First, feedback comes from tasks. Examples are tasks, such as doing a maths problem, writing, sawing wood or painting a surface. We observe our actions with varying degrees of accuracy and make adjustments much as a driver learns to steers a vehicle. Feedback on what is happening enables the driver to make decisions to steer in a particular direction. Sometimes during tasks we may even engage in self-talk (inside our head or verbalised to ourselves) in response to noticing what we are doing. The second source of feedback comes from people either through their expressions, actions or words. Some educational computer programs have encouraging responses built in as speech and text, such as 'Well done!' or 'Good try. Have another go.' The remaining feedback to children is likely to be written feedback as in the marking of work, grades and assessment marks. Little of this feedback is neutral in its effect on pupils' self-esteem, though much of it may not exactly be earth-shattering in its importance.

Tasks we do can invite a wide range of positive and negative feedback, feelings and responses. Depending on how any of us habitually copes with successes and failures, we can experience strong feelings about the task in relation to ourselves. We can feel very strongly positive or negative even before we start. As teachers we are not in control of how pupils themselves will respond, but we know from experience that tolerance of failure in individual pupils varies. More importantly, we have the chance to influence perceptions by the way we teach pupils to handle success and failure for themselves. Pupils' sense of themselves is at stake. In an ideal world teachers could boost each pupil's self-esteem on a daily basis, and some teachers believe they can actually do this. In my ideal world, pupils would become far better at recognising success and boosting self-esteem for themselves. They already have strong needs to be approved by their friends and teachers, as most pupils do. The need for well-handled positive feedback from teachers cannot be underestimated, but it need not create dependency or generate an even greater need for praise.

Realistically there is no guarantee that as teachers we can always remember to describe pupil progress positively. We might learn to give positive comments to pupils, but we cannot always guarantee to do this every time. Pupils have some responsibility for praising themselves. I have heard teachers talk about their pupils needing 'to take responsibility for themselves' and 'take responsibility for their learning'. Too often, this can be misunderstood as a need to blame ourselves when things go wrong. Seligman (1990) is quick to point out that self-blame leads directly to low self-esteem, and can become an established reaction to failure. Self-esteem depends largely on the perceptions and feelings we have about events and ourselves in relation to others. It does not depend on the events that happen, so much as the way in which we view them. Pupils, for example, may have irrational perceptions of failing to achieve a high enough standard, or not getting close enough to a view of success they imagined. A gap between how anyone sees themselves achieving and an ideal is in some ways healthy for human development. Without aspirations towards ideals we could become passive and no longer strive for anything.

Pupils who continually blame themselves can see themselves as being worthless, unlovable and stupid. Pupils who find reasons to blame external factors are, according to Seligman, simply protecting their self-esteem. He admits this is healthy enough for them, but not very helpful for us if we are trying to teach pupils whose view of learning is very negative. They may habitually blame themselves for their lack of ability ('I'm useless at doing science', 'I'm not talented') or blame external factors ('I couldn't see the board', 'He/she kept interrupting me', 'This is boring/a waste of time'). Although we may describe them as having low self-esteem, this is actually an overgeneralisation. A point made by McKay and Fanning (1992) is that low self-esteem, although thought of as a general state of being, actually relates to more specific situations. At school a child may have low self-esteem regarding academic ability, but at home higher self-esteem resulting from skill at playing computer games. Another pupil might feel they are good at schoolwork, but have low self-esteem about being a member of a group and socialising outside school. Levels of self-esteem also fluctuate according to how we perceive events affecting us for good or ill.

Most of the time individuals quite reasonably assume that the way they view events, relationships and themselves are accurate because there needs to be some basis for making day-to-day decisions. Where perceptions are negative, Martin Seligman (1990) and Harriet Braiker (1989) both offer strategies for changing them. Any accompanying negative devaluing self-talk, inside their heads, can be changed to a more positive dimension. Perceptions and beliefs, they claim, can change as we learn to think and talk about them differently. I will develop the educational context of their ideas and provide practical examples in the chapters which follow.

Remaining positive, and being aware of when we are negative, requires that we practise the classroom language to achieve this. In the heat of the moment things can still be different because feelings of frustration and tiredness take over. Teachers are fallible, not super-human. Like people in other jobs, they need a good old moan with a colleague now and again. Sharing difficult experiences with others is a way of getting a sense of meaning back into our world.

> I know all the theory. I know I need to step back from the situation and try to pick out strengths. I know I need to be patient and positive. But I got wound up with this kid Darren didn't I? He was fiddling with his pen and talking as I looked at his work. He was supposed to understand division in maths and I must have told them a million times to carry the remainder over. This time I'd arrived late at school because the car wouldn't start and I was already a bit angry and fed up, so I shouted at him, which I knew I shouldn't have done. 'What do you think you're doing? No. Let's get real! What are you NOT doing that you should know how to by now?' – all the things I didn't want to hear coming out of my mouth. 'How many times have I told you to carry figures over? Eh? How many times? Don't think of showing me that until you've sorted it out properly, you hear me?' Screaming pitch? Almost. The weird thing is I could hear myself saying all the wrong things but I couldn't switch to a calmer, more positive exchange. I'd had enough of it and it felt like it was somebody else talking, and could hear myself saying inside my head, 'Cool it. Don't say it. Don't say it.' But I still said it didn't I?
> (Primary-school teacher)

We might know in our minds that negative critical comment is deadly to self-esteem, but it is another matter framing our words more positively to counteract this. The gap between theory and practice closes slowly. As teachers, we can catch ourselves being negative when we would rather be positive. We are human and we fail. Beyond the failures, there are changes we can try to make in what we habitually say and do in the classroom. If this seems difficult to achieve, we might remember that a similar process already happens for many teachers at the start of their careers. They change their classroom language and action as they discover what effect their comments seem to have on children. How can this process be extended to develop a positive framework for improvement, without ignoring the reality of pupils' errors and failures? My experience is that teaching is a profession where the practice of correcting errors and saying 'what is wrong' is deeply ingrained. Of necessity, we are adept at noticing what goes wrong and trying to do something about it. Criticism and correction are after all part and parcel of teaching. Fortunately there are ways to redirect negative classroom language to something more constructive and positive than it often is. Seligman (1990), and Rogers (1992) both agree that redirection of this kind is difficult to achieve, but still possible and certainly worth learning.

In any situation, we have underlying automatic responses that quickly surface. The automatic responses tend to be buried within our style of explaining our lives, and they do not easily become dislodged. We have internal self-talk that can tell us something 'should' or 'shouldn't' have happened or that 'we ought to be able to cope by now' or that something should be better than it is. We compare how things are with how we think they 'ought to be' or 'should be' and turn the difference into negative criticism. An important ingredient in developing positive teaching is understanding the relationship between automatic self-talk and our perceptions. Any proposed changes to what we say, described in the following chapters, will inevitably include changes to self-talk. Reactions to tasks and events can be driven by highly emotional self-talk as pupils and teachers feel frustrated and disappointed, elated or excited ('It's just not fair!', 'I must get it right', 'I'm really bad at this', 'I liked doing that', 'It's fantastic!'). The extent to which we ourselves can be aware of our negative responses varies as do our emotions. As Rogers says, we cannot choose our emotions, but we can choose our perceptions of classroom events, and the way we attribute success and failure.

If we want to be positive in the classroom, the quality of feedback we give or receive matters. The way it is interpreted through self-talk lies at the heart of positive exchange in the classroom. If a teacher's good lesson plans and subject knowledge are a prerequisite for effective teaching, then feedback is the fuel. We may talk of giving feedback as 'constructive criticism' or feedback intended to boost an individual's self-esteem. I include the teacher's self-esteem in this too, because without teaching being rewarding it is difficult to give continually of ourselves. One of the hardest things for a teacher to do is to be positive when giving feedback on failure. It is sometimes much harder for some teachers to cope with than recognising success. Failure can diminish, or alternatively provide a positive springboard for learning. Feedback on failure can be threatening or promising, and it takes a skilful teacher to know the difference.

For the teacher, feedback from pupils can be a facial expression, a child's negative frown of confusion or a positive moment of understanding conveyed by wide-eyed delight. There is also the reality of experiencing negative and aggressive feedback from pupils who are 'acting out' and intend to be disruptive. Some of the best teachers I know are actually brilliant self-correctors as they respond to children. They do not ignore difficulties. They read the classroom situation accurately and have the ability to change direction according to the feedback they receive and the signals they give. They watch out for misunderstandings, self-correct their explanations, and have some idea of the effect they have on pupils. Their skill is one of trying to minimise possible difficulties and avoid laying psychological landmines for children to step on. The very best teachers can make learning feel achievable and fun without lowering expectations or reducing the value of tasks. If these attributes seem to fit almost every teacher in the world, we are back again with the familiar. Beyond the familiar is the possibility that some teachers are exceptionally good at this and we can learn something from them.

We might think that to teach positively means going overboard with the praise and encouragement that we give to children. Few teachers would disagree with the general view that praise is necessary and powerful in keeping the ethos of a classroom positive. As Dreikurs and Cassel (1972) put it, 'A child needs encouragement like a plant needs water.' The difficulties with sustaining praise and encouragement are that not every problem can be solved by being encouraging. Being encouraging in the face of continual negative pupil behaviour, such as a pupil being sullen and muttering snide comments, can be very draining. Praise that encourages has to be believed by pupils or it is worthless. It can otherwise make children doubt the praiser (Faber and Mazlish 1980). Something else is needed, because some feedback about errors is unavoidably going to be negative, so praising effort may be no compensation whatever for failure. Over-praising, as McKay and Fanning (1992) comment, can make children feel uncomfortable because they know that they are not actually 'brilliant', 'the cleverest', 'most generous' pupils in the world.

Recognising cycles of failure

There are some children in every class who may have already made up their minds that things are not going to work for them. They have become negative despite their teacher's attempts at enthusiastic encouragement. Previous experience influences how they feel about learning anything new or difficult. Those pupils who have had success in the past can risk trying something new, because if they fail, they have a bank-balance of previous success on which to draw. They can afford to take the knocks and try again. Other pupils are tenacious by nature and will try again regardless of setbacks. By contrast, the pupil who readily says, 'This is stupid, I don't want to do it' is really saying that they have had enough or that they cannot face failing. It is likely that they are saying to themselves, 'I'm stupid. I'm afraid that I can't do it', responses which can lead to their exhibiting silence at one extreme and acting out mischievously at the other. As far as the task at hand is concerned, they minimise failure by minimising their emotional investment in the task (Solomon 1992: 58). If there is a prophecy in the classroom, it is that there will be certain children locked into patterns of behaviour in which they are not going to experience academic success. Pupils, for example, who do not really want to be involved at the start of lessons have no strong reason to listen to any instructions there happen to be. A common pattern is: not listening, therefore not really understanding, and consequently experiencing failure with the tasks that are set. Tasks then become a chore, and the prize for failure may be that the teacher sets a much simpler, but even less interesting task. The cycle continues as experiences demotivate children and any previous willingness to be involved dissipates.

This cycle of failure naturally pushes pupils into finding other ways to survive the school day. Some will become expert at surviving their day by doing the minimum, manipulating teachers into giving them extra attention and wasting time. If children have low academic self-esteem, the chances are that instead of involving themselves in tasks, they already rely on other strategies to feel important. What teacher has not experienced children being a disruptive distraction, calling out and wandering across the room? The pay-off for them is probably to be stopped and for attention and peer approval to be directed their way. Other familiar patterns persist. Give or take a few moments of apparent willingness, some pupils always want to do something else instead of what they or their teacher had agreed to do. They may even have had a say in how the task would be done, agreed they would make a start, but soon found a more attractive distraction. This can be anything from asking irrelevant questions of others to repairing pens, pencil cases, arranging equipment, or even finishing another task they thought they needed to. The alternatives to remaining on-task are endlessly subversive. The possibilities for pupils gaining undeserved attention are what can make teaching so difficult at times.

Concerning failure, Seligman (1990) has described a state he calls 'learned helplessness', where some people become convinced that whatever they do it will make no difference. Their low tolerance of difficulty and failure (in their own eyes) ensures that experience after experience reinforces their belief that they cannot influence or have any control over their lives. They learn to be helpless. What Seligman claims happens is that whenever they feel that they have failed, their belief about failure strongly influences their next try. Further failure pushes them towards anticipating that the next thing they try will inevitably fail too. After several 'failures', they become convinced that their lack of ability pervades far more areas of their life than it actually does. Their beliefs about themselves become very negative and are described by them as being permanent, using such generalised statements as 'I'm useless', 'I'm hopeless at doing this'. Instead of seeing difficulties as temporary and specific to the situation, they see them as permanent weaknesses. They then stop trying and see themselves as incapable of success, which of course becomes self-fulfilling as they close off any possibility of its ever happening. Plan B soon goes into operation. Alternatives to making the effort surface, and almost any distraction or withdrawn behaviour is possible. For success to be experienced a minimum requirement is genuine involvement. Seligman's interest is in why some people still try in the face of extreme adversity rather than giving up. More promising still are ideas about how optimism can be learned (Chapter 2).

What of the way we explain failure to pupils? The educational consultant Bill Rogers describes a near disaster when he was trying to learn how to sail:

> The best teacher I ever had never ever criticised my failures, but he *did* acknowledge them. I was learning to sail and I capsized early on. He came alongside my boat and said, 'The boat's in the drink, Bill. The sail's in the water now, but when you climbed up onto the hull . . . ', and he's saying this from a little dinghy and I'm coughing and spluttering in the water. 'Bill, you climbed straight back and you remembered your overboard drill.' He repeated it, 'You remembered your overboard drill.' I felt secure with that guy teaching me. First of all I felt better about the capsizing and in feeling better, you do better. Although I felt bad about capsizing, I didn't feel *so* bad. Then he said, 'Do you know what to do next?' and I said, 'Gee, I think so', and he said, 'When you're pulling the centreboard down just let it settle a few moments and then climb back into the boat and point the sail into the wind.' You see, he didn't concentrate on my failures, yet the failure was very powerful as learning experience. But the failure didn't diminish me in any way.
>
> (Interview, 1997)

How does negative thinking feed on itself?

I have so far sketched how some pupils can be locked into cycles of negativity, experiencing failure and helplessness. These are extreme examples and most individuals manage to be something other than helpless. Extreme examples are useful for beginning to understand how positive and negative responses can feed the cycle of success or failure. Failure can breed failure unless the cycle is broken. Suzie Orbach (1997) illuminates the extreme attractions of negativity. She talks about a person's loss of motivation and state of hopelessness as well as their helplessness.

> It is much trickier to help when hopelessness has become an individual's signature. All their experience is filtered through a channel of defeatism or of purposelessness. Nothing works out, and when it *does*, when opportunities arise and things get better, they can find it very hard to adapt. It's as though there is something safe in negativity. It's known. It's stable. It's reliable.
>
> (Orbach 1997)

There are similarities to be drawn between her comments and times when teachers try to help pupils who are seriously unmotivated. Whatever the teacher suggests is turned down as being pointless in a 'can't do', 'waste of time', 'won't work' style of negative avoidance response, which is the opposite of an involved 'could try this'. As Orbach describes, the cycle of negative experience feeding negativity can lead to a personal style which is hard for some people to give up. The negativity has become a habit, practised, familiar and a reassuringly self-protective filter.

Safety in negativity can be addictive. The pupil or teacher who says 'I'm no good at this' is relatively safe from possible criticism or the effects of failure because they have already declared their incompetence. Nobody can say worse if we have already said the worst about ourselves. In high-achieving individuals, 'It's not up to my usual standard' can be the more subtle form of negativity. Negative comment and negative thinking protect us from what we most fear, whether it is fear of failure, fear of humiliation, fear of criticism or fear of rejection by other people (Humphreys 1996). We protect our self-esteem in whatever we do and say, sometimes intentionally annoying, even wounding other people in the process. As Humphreys explains, by labelling ourselves extremely as 'hopeless', or 'no good' at something, we reduce our own expectations of ourselves so that possible failure is not such a hammer-blow. Whenever we say to other people, 'I'm useless at . . . ', it reduces their expectations of us by leading them to believe that only mistakes and failures can be expected of us.

Negative comments are a fast track to making us feel better about underlying fears of failure. By labelling others or their efforts as 'no good, abysmal' or 'dreadful' we also protect our self-esteem by affirming our sense of superiority. Negative comments about people and events can sometimes make us feel more effective and competent by virtue of comparison. Knowing this, of course, may make little difference because it seems to be a basic human mechanism for releasing our feelings of frustration. It is often a way of reaffirming belief in ourselves.

The attraction of avoiding failure is not confined to children. It is obvious to most of us, even if we think we learn from our failures, that we would rather avoid them. Similarly attractive to some pupils is avoidance of doing anything, a state which is passive, a focus of no action, and no effort. In the classroom, it may take the form of passive resistance as a pupil privately decides not to be involved. There can be a mental 'sit this one out' barrier to taking part in most things. Staffrooms can also be places where tensions, often between two or three individuals, produce such negativity. This can be seen in a teacher's negative avoidance comments in a staff planning meeting. Familiar defences are remarks like 'We did that five years ago and it didn't work then', 'That never works', 'Why change it now?', 'Well, we already do that, don't we?' Negative tone of voice also colours comments of a relatively neutrally worded kind so that they then sound defensive or aggressively negative in tone.

Whenever anything goes wrong in the classroom, and of course it frequently does, we have little control over how we react emotionally. Experience of teaching helps us to understand classroom disasters, but the level of emotional frustration, anger or fear is actually unpredictable. Plans that go wrong, conflicts of staff interest, and pupils who underachieve or misbehave can fuel our emotions. Pupils too respond emotionally. Negative emotions can centre on their fear of feeling stupid, being made an example of, or experiencing failure again and again. John-Roger McWilliams and Peter McWilliams (1991) describe negative reactions as our fight-or-flight response to feelings of anger or fear. Our *fight* (anger, including anger with ourselves) causes us to complain and find fault. Our *flight* (fear, and underconfidence) causes us to give up and abandon things. The mind when in fight mode becomes strongly addicted to the psychological 'high' of being right in finding fault. I have experienced this fight/flight response myself in the context of teaching children as well as from a personal point of view. I can imagine it from the child's perspective too. They explain:

> How does negative thinking work? When the fight or flight response is triggered we *look for everything that is wrong*. And there's always *something* wrong, so our mind filters out the positive and focuses on the negative . . . the chain reaction is to be enthusiastically negative, which in turn triggers even more hideous evidence, which kicks off an even stronger fight or flight response. Get the idea? Triggering the fight or flight response actually puts enormous stress on the body. The trouble is that the mind tries to find reasons for the fight/flight response . . . and there will *always* be something to be found.
>
> (McWilliams and McWilliams 1991: 31)

Fight/flight responses rapidly accumulate. Frustration can lead to negative thinking, next to complaint and criticism and in turn to the next frustration, until we are almost at screaming pitch. One thing out of place triggers more and yet more. Teachers generally want children to behave in ways they find acceptable and want to establish social routines, politeness and consideration for others. Children – most children – have needs other than being polite and remembering to put things away. They want to do things like go out to play, eat lunch and talk to friends. A common trigger for frustration for anyone, including children, is to know what we already want to do, be ready to do it, then have to do something else. A short-cut to protecting ourselves, and thereby trying to head off yet more fight/flight feelings, is to become negative. In the classroom a teacher can hardly withdraw, be negative and unresponsive. It may not even be very healthy psychologically, but experienced teachers will step back daily from their negative classroom frustrations to maintain an outward semblance of sanity. The inner stress this can create is well known.

For some individuals, negative thoughts and critical comments can feed negativity because they are convincing. Negative comments, especially about ourselves and our apparent mismatch in achievement, are *believable*. If we can always find something wrong in the fight/flight response, then we can always find something convincingly critical to say about ourselves. Various reasons are advanced for this, but the most common is that as children we experienced considerable importance and attention attached to behaviour parents did *not* want. We also experienced significant negative critical comment when we did not come up to expectations. There is a certain familiarity for us in being reminded of the criticisms of childhood. I have frequently asked myself why student teachers find it so hard to believe praise for their teaching. It is as if the inner voice of a parent says, 'That's not true. Don't be so stupid. There are far better teachers than you! You're only starting teaching so how can you possibly be any good at it?' The shortcomings (there are always some) are there to prevent us from deserving the praise. Somewhere, the teaching fell short of perfection, short of how it 'should have been' and the difference cancelled out what was achieved.

I am not suggesting that negative comments can be eradicated from teaching and learning. Inevitably, pupils who go against agreed classroom rules, for example, and fall far short of reasonable expectations will experience negative comment. They may even experience punishment. In the short term this may solve any immediate problems of disruption, but how effective is it over a period of time? Derek Rollinson (1997) has concluded that within the workplace treating people in a negative way has little improving effect. Summarising his research findings, the *Observer* newspaper ran a headline in February 1997. This simply said, 'Treat 'em mean and they'll just be less keen.' Evidence showed that most disciplinary hearings for breaking the rules do not alter the behaviour of employees for the better. Where people had infringed company rules about time keeping or fiddled expenses they were disciplined. The effect of this was that they only grudgingly decided to conform. Many of them found the experience provoked resistance to conformity and some 45 per cent thought they would still continue to break the rules. Rollinson theorised that successful use of punishment requires very strict control of the surrounding conditions and this is extremely difficult to achieve.

A conclusion that may tentatively be drawn from this is that in the longer term, criticism and punishment militate against a culture like teaching, which actually depends on co-operation. If the research is anything to go by, all that happens is that trust is destroyed. Mistrust subsequently conditions how the individual views the workplace and the managers in it. An intriguing finding in Rollinson's research was that co-operation, and ownership of the problem, were involved in what he regarded as successful disciplinary procedures. As he explained, 'To be successful in improving an individual's behaviour, the manager has to get the person to admit they should not have broken the rule, and then ask them what they are going to do about it. So the person becomes the author of their own code of conduct.'

Positive thinking, switching focus

I began by describing how Sophie improved and how the story of her success has stayed with me. A question that remains is whether criticism and self-critical comment erode self-esteem or are simply a way of being realistic. When are negative thinking and criticism just the stark reality of the situation? Negative thinking may, as Humphreys reminds, be 'protective thinking', a way of defending self-esteem against possible or actual threat (Humphreys 1996). That sounds real enough. John-Roger McWilliams and Peter McWilliams (1991) are against positive thinking if it denies reality. So are Ellis (1994) and Seligman (1990). They are in favour of recognising disasters and difficulties, then switching focus to concentrate on the positive. They are against 'being positive' about everything in sight. The difference between positive thinking at all costs and switching focus from negative to positive is truly one of description. The emphasis on reality is exactly what the story of learning to sail exemplifies. The boat had capsized and the sail was in the water, but fortunately we remembered our overboard drill. The sailing teacher made no attempt to label or judge at the point of disaster. He simply described the reality and pulled the positive 'you remembered your overboard drill' into the foreground.

Learning to switch focus to concentrate on the positive has two stages, both of which are important for classroom practice. First, we learn that negative actions and reactions are often (though not always) individuals' ways of protecting themselves. Understanding that, we may grow to feel less personally threatened by their comments because they need not be taken at face value. Second, we can become better at looking for ways to describe success and failure, changing the negative critic for a healthier one. This is particularly important concerning perceptions of failure, since the effect on self-esteem can lead to passivity, anger or hopelessness. Thinking in a positive way can be difficult. Positive thoughts are there, but it is as if sometimes they are waiting for us to stop criticising long enough to hear them.

KEY POINTS

- Whatever difficulty appears, it is not permanent and pervasive, but specific and temporary.
- Positive teaching requires us to develop a 'high hope' factor for pupil success.
- Positive teaching is unlikely to be a matter of describing failures as successes, though it is certainly about pulling descriptions of success into the foreground.
- Positive teaching concerns the way we handle feedback, particularly negative feedback intended to draw attention to areas in need of improvement.
- Low self-esteem, although thought of as a general state of being, actually relates to more specific situations.

- Self-blame leads directly to low self-esteem.
- Negative thinking creates resentment if it is in the form of destructive criticism.
- Negative thinking threatens self-esteem, including our own.
- Negative actions and reactions are most probably an individual's way of protecting him- or herself.
- We can become better at looking for ways to describe success and failure, changing the negative critic for a more healthy one.

Chapter 2

Optimism learned in the classroom

One day in 1996 I asked my good and positive friend Professor Michael Berrill what he thought about optimism and pessimism. He replied,

> What's a pessimist's definition of hope? The feeling that the feeling you have will soon pass. I am certainly an optimist, and believe that optimism can be used as a force to make things happen. I also think the word 'optimist' is synonymous with 'fool'.

Maybe he was talking about recognising realities and not pretending there are no setbacks in life. The optimist has ways of seeing setbacks from a more encouraging point of view. Cognitive therapists believe that individuals can switch focus, redescribe and change their outlook to a more positive dimension (Bandler and Grinder 1979, 1982; Seligman 1990; Lindenfield 1995; Ellis 1962). At its simplest, the belief is that learning to dispute negative beliefs, and redescribe adverse events more positively, has the effect of changing how we feel. Against this view, Humphreys (1993) says that the way we see and describe things results from how we already feel about them, and negative critical comments are there to protect our self-esteem. Negative thoughts provide an essential means of making us less vulnerable by protecting us, so how can we possibly change them? According to Humphreys, the emotional vulnerabilities we already have precede the negative thought patterns. These views are partly reconciled in that both Humphreys and the group of cognitive therapists promote change through deliberately taking a more encouraging view of events and ourselves. Change is possible provided that the positive encouraging thoughts 'come from the gut' and are sincere (Humphreys 1993: 93). This is where the technique of redescribing involves a genuine switch of focus. If the word 'optimist' is synonymous with 'fool', it is when redescribing does not focus on finding genuinely positive aspects, but tries to pretend or invent a more positive picture where really none exists.

Why is learning to focus optimistically worth doing in the classroom? A strong reason is to promote perseverance in the face of difficulties. Positive perceptions are commonly associated with hope, tenacity and academic success (Seligman

1990; Nolen-Hoeksema *et al.* 1986). Negative perceptions are associated with passivity, low motivation and giving up easily. More importantly, a positive focus enables pupils to feel positive about their work. Consequently, they can be far more confident and rewarding to teach. Compared with those who are negative, willing pupils are likely to achieve more and can be a positive influence on others in the classroom. They are working because they want to, and the experience can have a reinforcing effect on how they feel about academic tasks. In addition, learning to focus positively can help pupils to cope with setbacks, so they deal with criticism and failure more easily. Positive teachers I have observed seem to be able to transmit their optimism and create a climate of belief in success. I cannot prove this because there are so many other factors involved in success, such as good planning, worthwhile targets, accurate feedback and clear explanations. I am convinced that focusing on the positive affects pupils' willingness to give of their best and believe in themselves. The positive classroom is one of possibilities, rather than the constraints of a humdrum daily grind. Criticising and describing negatively can be so energy sapping and purposeless. Generating a positive classroom ethos can spiral outwards to affect pupils, who in turn become more positive towards their studies. The spiral of energised teaching and learning is at times almost tangible.

Seligman (1990) takes the view that we do not begin life thinking negatively, but have learned to do so. Consequently we can learn to recognise self-sabotaging attitudes and change them for more useful ones. The general idea is that children can learn to do this for themselves, provided there is input from their teachers. Seligman simply calls this process 'learned optimism'. His approach, and many other cognitive strategies, have their origins in the work of Albert Ellis (1962). In the 1960s, Ellis radically changed ideas about negative and depressive thinking, which he called 'stupid behaviour on the part of nonstupid people'. He took the view that individuals need not indulge in blame, particularly self-blame, and make irrational rules and demands for themselves. Instead they could learn to focus positively on trying to correct or improve in the future. This was not an attempt to stop people accepting responsibility for their mistakes and misdeeds. On the contrary, Ellis proposed that individuals took responsibility for creating their own problems, rather than blaming external circumstances. He pointed out that negatively criticised individuals tended to focus compulsively on their errors when there were far better ways to function. They 'illogically upset themselves' by their distorted thinking. Not only that, they inhabited a self-created world of unreasonable expectations, self-blame and barriers to their own progress.

Ellis's philosophy holds that the vast majority of human beings do not sufficiently accept themselves as fallible and error-prone. They often try to be superhuman, and discover they cannot be. They fall short of their unrealistic ideas and so denigrate themselves. This results in having a low tolerance for the inescapable foibles of others and themselves. Consequently, they magnify their feelings of disappointment, sorrow and regret to become less appropriate feelings of frustration, self-pity, worry and anxiety. They make unreasonable perfectionist demands about how their lives should be, continually wanting to prove themselves, rather than just being themselves. This needless and anxiety-prone thinking takes them into several cul-de-sacs of negative thought about their own worth and ability. Over the years, Ellis has demonstrated that there are ways to understand ourselves differently by abandoning self-defeating thought patterns. Although events have an influence on our lives, Ellis claims that we choose certain beliefs about them and, by changing some of our more irrational beliefs, we will change how we feel.

I have drawn particularly on the work of Ellis and Seligman to translate some of these strategies for more direct use in the classroom. They fit classroom situations well because they are realistic, do not ignore emotions and are simple to use. In summary, Ellis and Seligman's approach is to challenge *distorted* negative beliefs. These are then redescribed in a more positive way. The aim of the strategies described here is to adjust some of the negative classroom distortions to more realistic beliefs. Five steps in developing this positive focus in the classroom are important:

1 Recognising automatic negative responses.
2 Learning to dispute negative responses.
3 Reframing negative perceptions more positively.
4 Learning a practical strategy to enhance this.
5 Teaching pupils to do the same.

Recognising automatic negative responses

Negative responses to adverse events can surface almost before we, or our pupils, are aware of them. Teaching is a job where, even when things are going well, we are often on the lookout for the situation falling apart. We want teaching to have successful outcomes and we spend some time thinking about the possible pitfalls. This might seem like being pre-programmed to see what goes wrong, but it is actually an attempt to steer teaching and learning along the best possible course. In that sense, negativity is not a disease in which every symptom must be eradicated in search of a cure. Negative reactions and critical comments are signals that tell us we might make adjustments and switch focus. We will still hear pupils and teachers say that things are 'disastrous', 'hopeless', 'awful' and 'useless'. We will still have days when we feel that everything is falling apart. Learning to handle these negative responses is more important than obsessively trying to remove them, even if we could.

We can change our responses if we understand what they are and how they are created. Automatic negative responses are the result of habits of thought and feeling. The automatic thoughts we have tend to be short phrases or sentences, so well-practised that they can go unchallenged (Seligman 1990: 89). A common automatic response for some children, and a good number of teachers, is that whatever the lesson, or whatever the work, the outcome could *always* have been better. Extreme examples are if we or our pupils habitually, frequently and automatically mutter negative criticism to ourselves, such as 'hopeless', 'no good', 'not good enough', 'stupid' and other more emotive labels. Frequently used negative responses are those which judge the worth of events and people adversely against a personal belief. This may result in negative language (often internalised as pupil or teacher self-talk) such as 'waste of effort', 'took too long', 'should know by now', and labels such as 'useless', 'pathetic', 'slow', 'bad', 'worse', 'terrible' and 'disaster'. Questions are a common form of negative self-talk as in 'What's the point?' and 'Why on earth do I bother?'

Teachers may recognise certain pupils' automatic negative responses better than their own, especially when the moans, grumbles and disruptions become predictable. Even when we are aware of automatic negative responses, teaching is one of those jobs where sometimes we bite our tongue and appear calm when actually we feel critical, angry or stressed.

Emotional tolerance of pupil actions is often stretched to the limit when we know that getting frustrated in front of pupils may not help matters. Sometimes displaying anger helps, but teaching is an occupation where the psychological temperature of the classroom needs to be borne in mind. We may let off steam later in the school staffroom, but we try to stay reasonably calm in front of a class. We are not alone in this because pupils also find themselves in situations where they have to do things against their wishes. Some may decide to be negative in advance so as to protect themselves from disappointment. There is obvious safety for any individual in predicting that something will not work, thereby creating an excuse not to try.

Automatic negative self-talk, the arch-critic inside our heads, can have a temporarily positive function. A critical voice can further aspirations to do better, so can be productive unless it gets out of hand. In its own words, it can tell us that we tried hard but could try a little harder, an aspiration we might find reasonable. Where it is least helpful, it automatically focuses on shortcomings from the immediate past set against some imagined ideal. It filters out the positive features in the quest for perfection. That perfection may focus on the imagined possible brilliance of a lesson, other teachers' or pupils' efforts, the way it went on a previous occasion – anything that pictures 'how it should have been for me'. The wasted emotion involved here arises from what I will call 'reminiscence fantasy'. This focuses on an imagined and ideal outcome, unrelated to what actually happened. This is something we all do from time to time as a buffer against disappointment. If reminiscence fantasy becomes prolonged, it is not very helpful.

There may be a personal pay-off in looking on the black side. Hooked into reminiscence fantasy, we can avoid facing the present reality. The distraction this offers might well be preferable to reality. Looking on the black side can also come closest at that moment to validating how we actually feel. We need first to let off steam, so reminiscing about how things might or should have been allows us to complain. We are perhaps sufficiently upset to draw negative conclusions from the misfit between what was and what might have been. What might have been is that someone else could or should have behaved differently (but they did not) or something should have happened (but did not happen). Reminiscence fantasy is attractive partly because responsibility and blame lie elsewhere. We can use it as a lever to persuade ourselves that someone else or something should fix things. We may also use it to reinforce a belief, such as being 'no good at maths'. The key issue for change lies in whether we can recognise negativity as an *automatic* response. Am I really no good at maths, or has part of this specific task on 'estimation' not worked for me today? Is the desire for 'how it should have been' automatic or a temporary, unrealistic and occasional wish?

It is worth remembering that some children seem to be born 'people-raters', continually making comparisons about themselves, parents and peers. By the age of 6, many children are prone to believe that the world revolves around them (Bernard and Joyce 1984: 112). This is a stage of development where it is extremely difficult for them to avoid the negative comments of parents. Their strong ideas about how the world should be can persist long into adulthood. McKay and Fanning (1992) trace some of the triggers for automatic negative responses to parental comments which were guaranteed to tear down a child's self-esteem. I treat these examples with some caution because everyone's childhood experience tends to be different. Parents, according to McKay and Fanning, may have overgeneralised by saying, 'You *always* do it wrong', 'You *never* think, do you?', '*All* you care about is yourself.' Children may also have heard, 'Your father *never* listens', 'You're *always* leaving your clothes around.' These all-pervasive comments emphasise behaviour as if it were a permanently negative trait and this can lead a child to feel hopeless about 'doing anything right'. There may have been additional vague parental threats such as 'Try that again and you'll see what happens', 'I'll break your neck if I see you do that again!' or, as a teacher recounted, 'If you break your legs climbing trees, don't come running to me.'

These comments are usually accompanied by a strongly negative tone of voice, and even aggressive shouting. Children learn that the parent is angry, and may even conclude that they themselves are bad and the cause of that anger. Older children learn that their parents are not seriously intending to break their necks, but younger children can be very intimidated by these threats (McKay and Fanning 1992: 253). Most negative comments brought from childhood un-wittingly label, judge, threaten or nag in some way. We can never really know how children interpret them because it is not possible to find out about everything that goes through a child's head when things go wrong.

Once internalised as an automatic response, negative classroom self-talk brought from childhood can be damaging. At worst, it can be self-talk as destructive as 'You can *never* do this so why try?', 'You're not really brainy. I don't know why you bother because it will only lead to disaster', 'You're stupid and you know it.' Lesser internal critics compare with others, 'You did OK, but not so well as David and Rachel', 'You can't finish things quickly like the rest of the class.' Where self-talk is expressed in a more personal way it may also change the pronoun to an 'I' as in 'I don't know why I bother, I can *never* finish this quickly enough.' This 'I' talk is self-blame and it is not hard to see that it may have begun as negative teacher-talk or parent-talk.

Self-talk can have a very positive outcome, as a Canadian colleague tells me. What I like about her story is the practical way she uses this.

> When I talk to people about self-talk, I frame it with the positive things that we know are happening and stress the individual's role in making those things happen. For example, 'You've just told me about electric currents and have perfectly described how to set up a parallel circuit. You need to remember that this is something you know and understand. So, if you are feeling a little overwhelmed about these problems, just remind yourself that you know this. Slow down. Back up, and go to those deep essentials that you know so well.'
>
> Must admit, I use self-talk when I'm feeling overwhelmed, which is probably much more often than some people might think. For us in the North Americas, it's *The Little Engine That Could*, a very popular children's book from long ago. I think I can, I think I can, I think I can . . . pretty hokey maybe, but powerful for lots of us.
>
> (Professor of Education)

Where are the strong signals for switching focus from negative to positive? Ellis (1962) realised that one of the most commonly found indicators of negative response is the unhealthy use of the word 'should' and its companions 'must', 'ought', 'should not', 'must not' and 'ought not'. There are, of course, justifiable 'shoulds' and 'oughts' that we use. There are potentially life-threatening situations such as drink driving. People *should not* drink and drive. We *should* feel angry from time to time if we are to allow anger its rightful place in our humanity. There are harmless 'shoulds' like 'I should get my hair cut tomorrow because my hair's long.' Pathological 'shoulds' are those derived from values and beliefs that are rigid and personal, often handed down through generations of parenting. An individual feels something *should* be different, better, or put back in a specific place and next finds the facts to fit the 'should'. This is particularly prominent in expressions of what people *must* do, or *should* have done, but did not. The feeling becomes the reality.

> It's not going to be helpful saying 'this *must* be' when it isn't. It is actually a denial of reality. It's like me going outside and saying 'It mustn't rain' when it rains. The universe is not going to stop it raining because I say it mustn't. It's annoying, but you might as well find a raincoat. Acknowledge the reality, even stressful reality, to put it in perspective. Otherwise you can get into self and other blame very quickly. Those global strong *musts*, *never*, *always* and *shoulds* will so dominate the situation. First, there's no way to recognise the possibilities for change. Second, it saps the will for change. That's the

problem, it really does sap the will. You're putting all your energy into self-defeating beliefs. A lot of people's self-defeating demands are entrenched, in the sense that they're embedded and produce habituated behaviour. It's easier to act on something embedded than to change it, and that's why when you hear someone saying 'I *never* get it right. I *should* have done . . . ' it's habituated. They don't really think about it any more. It came from somewhere, some time, at some point. Until they can consciously catch themselves saying these things, tuning into themselves, they close off from saying 'I forgot the worksheets today. That was a silly thing to do, but it doesn't make me a failure does it?' There's nothing wrong with deeply embedded thinking, unless it's global, generalised, determined and negative. The hard thing is to get people to be conscious of positive alternatives. It takes time.

(Bill Rogers, interview, 1997)

In the classroom it is not very helpful to keep reminding pupils not to use words like 'always', 'never', 'should' and 'must'. Pupils need to learn how global and inaccurate they are through understanding that there is not enough information in an 'always'. McKay and Fanning (1992) go so far as to say that pathological 'shoulds' are the destroyers of self-esteem. A lesson here for pupils is to begin to understand that they will not build their confidence with 'shoulds'. Behind an absolute such as 'never', 'always' or 'everyone', 'all', 'nobody' and 'nothing' can lurk the stock-in-trade rule of the perfectionist and critic. Find an absolute and we will probably also find a demanding 'should'. Conversely, find a 'should' and we will find an absolute rooted in beliefs and values. Notice in the following examples how permanent and pervasive, global and generalised they are:

I *always* get it wrong (I *should not* get it wrong).

I have to do *everything* myself (somebody else *ought to* offer help).

I *never* want help (I *should* be totally self-reliant).

Nothing ever works around here (things *must not* break down).

That *should not* have happened (things *should always* be right).

That *should not* be put there (things *should always* be in place).

I *should not* make that mistake (I'm *never* allowed to fail).

I *should not* eat this (I *must always* be thin).

The mind easily becomes addicted to the belief of being right about what should or should not be. As John-Roger McWilliams and Peter McWilliams (1991) comment about this addiction, there is an emotional pay-off about being right. They point out, 'In a far less than perfect world, one of the easiest ways to be right is to predict failure.' An underlying, even subconscious prediction of failure allows us to say, 'I/they should never have done that.' In a perfect world mistakes do not happen and things are put in their rightful place. Add to that a few generalisations, 'always', 'shoulds' and 'should-nots', and we have a recipe for classroom frustration and negativity. The critic was right after all and our compensation lies in having predicted it. If we want to be right, all we need do is construct a mind's view of possible perfection and look for the shortcomings. The question missing from the tyranny of 'shoulds' is 'What universal law says it should be like that?' As Ellis argued, 'shoulds' occur because what we tell ourselves is an inflexible rule in the first place. We hang on doggedly to groundless beliefs when there is not one iota of evidence to back them up.

What chance is there for the teacher who is inevitably by profession a corrector of errors and upholder of standards? We can rationalise by saying that as teachers we need to have high standards, therefore our criticisms are justified. A personal pay-off for 'should' and 'ought' is that from time to time perfectionism is temporarily rewarded. Most of the time perfectionism leads to failure, but once in a while everything works out and there is a minor miracle. Temporarily we can achieve as near perfection as we hoped, so much so that we are locked into the buzz of wanting the next pay-off (McKay and Fanning 1992: 24). The frustration between pay-offs for perfectionism seems a price worth paying. The truth is that our high standards, when related to 'shoulds', are unrealistic and inflexible demands. These demands will not change reality, but they can and do create stress (Rogers 1992: 14).

An alternative is to see them as preferences about which we may find agreement with some but not all other teachers. Healthy expressions of high standards, needs and desires can be more realistically stated with less pressure. The automatic thought 'I *should not* have made that mistake' is of course reminiscence fantasy. Here are some preferences in the present reality.

> I *prefer* not to make that mistake (which I made).
>
> I *prefer* to have that put back in place (when it wasn't).
>
> I would *prefer* to have had help (when nobody helped).
>
> I *would like* that to work (and it's not working at the moment).
>
> I *prefer* not to put on weight (so choose whether to eat that).
>
> I *prefer* to do this myself (but sometimes need help).
>
> I *prefer* to be really thorough (even when I'm not).

Ellis (1994), for his part, holds that flexible preferences are at the very core of psychological well-being. Dryden (1996) makes the additional point that preferences need to be stated in full or there is a good chance that they will imply a 'should' or a 'must'. A fully stated preference which is free of this implication would be 'I want to pass my driving test, *but* I don't have to' (Dryden 1996: 4).

The word 'want' in this instance is a substitute for 'prefer'. An implied 'should' arises when there is a half-statement such as 'I prefer to be really thorough', implying 'and I really *must* be thorough, come what may, and I *will* be thorough come what may'.

An objection to turning demands into preferences is that certain things have deadlines. They *must* be done, therefore cannot possibly be preferences. It is not much use saying 'I prefer to have this essay in on time, but won't'. Ellis responds to this by pointing out that it is still a preference, but there are of course consequences for all actions we take.

> Certainly we could use this as an excuse to procrastinate as can almost any other idea be used by rationalising people. The mere fact that something is a strong preference means that it doesn't have to be acceded to, but that one will get bad results if it is not.
>
> (Albert Ellis, email to author, 1998)

If we see preferences as demands, they will have stressful consequences because they are fixed. Failure to fulfil them can generate anger and a sense of guilt.

There is one more important feature to notice about the preferences expressed in these examples. They are mainly 'I' statements, firmly putting the preference into a personal arena. It is no longer the case that things outside myself *should* be otherwise, but that 'I prefer' them to be otherwise. The 'I' statement, in this case, allows us to take some responsibility for how we feel. The 'I' statements of preference are very different from the 'I' statements of self-blame. 'I *should*' is a demand on the self. Nowhere in the preferences will we find 'I *should* get it right' or 'I *always* get it wrong'. The main advantages of 'I' preferences, rather than 'I' rigid demands, are that we are likely to be less put out when things go wrong, and less justified in blaming anyone for what happens. There is less chance of running ourselves down with critical labels.

The ultimate inflexibility would be to say that we *should not* use the word 'should' or that we *should always* substitute the words 'I prefer'. When we are aware of these in the language we use and hear, it is not a chance to beat ourselves over the head for forgetting there are healthy alternatives. The effort of avoiding all 'shoulds' is frankly not worth the anxiety. Unless we notice rather than look for 'shoulds', the intellectual analysis can paralyse communication. Mind would no longer hit muscle as we ceased to be acting spontaneously in our communications. If we begin to believe that the 'shoulds' and 'nevers' we use mean we are being unrealistic, the next stage is to find out if we are.

Learning to dispute negative responses

Learning to dispute automatic responses is a matter of marshalling contrary evidence against underlying negative beliefs (Seligman 1990: 89). Its effect, according to well-researched examples, is to change negative feelings and perceptions so that the consequences are better. We actually feel better by being less stressed. Beliefs we might dispute typically take the form of distortions in thinking, described by therapists as 'cognitive distortions'. Once we can recognise distortions for what they are, we can redescribe our beliefs in more realistic and positive terms. Clues to distortion so far mentioned include reminiscence fantasy, and the use of absolutes such as 'always', 'never', 'everyone', and 'nobody'. These absolutes identify the cognitive distortion of overgeneralisation (McKay and Fanning 1992: 58; Howie 1997: 61). They close the doors of possibility because there is no specific information about the circumstances in which the overgeneralisation arose. 'Brainy', 'stupid' and 'failure' are similarly global labels that carry too little detail.

An initial stage in disputing will be to recognise that individuals may genuinely feel stupid, always wrong or a failure. Feelings need to be validated, but the beliefs underlying them challenged. Individuals are not permanently, for all time, 'brilliant' or 'stupid'. They are not pervasively, in all possible circumstances, 'brilliant' or 'stupid'. As frustrated expressions at the time, the use of such labels is sometimes understandable, but these need to be disputed for their lack of specific evidence. Choosing the moment to do this with pupils is not easy because of the immediate need to feel understood for feeling stupid. One way to dispute absolutes such as 'always', 'nobody', 'never', 'ever', and labels such as 'stupid' is to repeat them back. They are usually such exaggerations that repeating them can soon reveal that they are ridiculous. Some individuals would stick to their guns to be difficult, but many would see the exaggerations for what they are. By repeating back, we allow pupils to realise for themselves, rather than having it spelled out letter by letter.

I have deliberately omitted any indication of who begins speaking, in the following examples, to allow for self-talk as well as pupil–teacher talk. Verbalising, even to ourselves, can reveal the ridiculous provided that voice-tone is sympathetic rather than sarcastic or aggressive. Sometimes it is enough to repeat back the generalisation and pause to allow contrary evidence to surface. If a long pause does not change anything, a more specific direction or question can help. No attempt to mimic sarcastically will be of use here. The more genuinely serious the repetition, the more ridiculous.

EXPOSITION:
We *never* do *anything* interesting in this school.

REPETITION:
We *never* do *anything* even remotely interesting. [PAUSE]
Well, it's true some things are not so interesting.
What was interesting, even if it was ages ago?

EXPOSITION:
Nothing I do *ever* goes right.

REPETITION:
No. Absolutely *nothing ever*. [PAUSE]
Sometimes it feels like that. Describe just one moment
when everything worked out.

Some pupils will even laugh at themselves after the pause. Others may offer corrections, such as saying, 'Well, maybe there are some things we do that are interesting.' Others will resist outwardly, but may well privately rethink.

Further negative distortions come as polarised thinking. This generalisation happens when we habitually judge something as being either a success or a failure, good or bad, brilliant or disastrous, right or wrong, but nothing between these extremes. Clues in the language are the way we label, such as 'But it's an absolute disaster', 'It's really bad.' There is no middle way of greys between the extremes of black and white because that is how it feels. Actual evidence of there being any other possibility is therefore absent. Again, a technique for disputing is to repeat back the generalisation. Serious adult voice-tone is important because taking the generalisation very seriously is paradoxically what reveals it as ridiculous.

EXPOSITION:
This is a complete and utter *failure*.

REPETITION:
Yes, a complete and utter *failure*. [PAUSE]
In what way a failure? Am I leaving out something here?
What's missing that would describe some parts as more successful?

EXPOSITION:
This is *stupid*.

REPETITION:
Yes, this is *stupid*. [PAUSE]
In what way is it *stupid*?
What positive aspects are being excluded here?

Some distorted thinking falls into the category of mind-reading and personalisation (McKay and Fanning 1992: 62). This works on the false premise that other people think in the way we do, therefore we can trust our intuition and make assumptions about what they think and feel. Mind-reading results in comments like 'She knows I'm not good at this and that's what is making her angry', 'She thinks I'm slow', 'He did that because he thinks I'm not pulling my weight.' Pupils who distort may also mind-read from previous experience: 'I hated this last time, so I know why she doesn't want to help me.' Personalised distorted thinking is where the individual thinks that all comments in some way refer to them, especially the criticisms. The thought is that the teacher who complained that we did not work hard enough must have been referring to 'me'. The disappointment about how the class behaved means 'it's my fault'. Sometimes the personalised thinking is emotional in origin. The individual feels emotionally very down, so almost any comment is felt to refer to them whether it does or not. Mind-reading also includes assumptions made from a frown or facial expression assumed to signal disapproval. This has its roots in the way we experienced disapproval in childhood and the way we signal it ourselves. Some frowns do of course disapprove, but this is not sufficient basis for mind-reading.

Distortions have two things in common. They lack substantial evidence, or their evidence is suspect. Fortunately the more global, generalised and all-pervasive is the belief, the more obvious its flaws can be. Key statements to use in disputing for ourselves are to say: 'No, that's not true because . . . ' or 'I'm probably off track in thinking that because . . . '. Here are two examples of pupils' disputations, which begin with a global generalisation.

> I'm *hopeless* at sport. No, that's not true because I was once in a display team and we did well at gymnastics, and gymnastics is a sport. I'm not very skilled in football or cricket maybe, but I can enjoy a game of tennis with somebody about the same level as I am. And I have played cricket. It's true I don't really like playing team games, but I joined a tennis club for a while and that was good fun. Sport is maybe not my best thing, but I do swim twice a week and that's something isn't it? I won't be rushing past the winning post and doing a four-minute mile, but it's not true to say I'm hopeless. I'm enjoying the sport I do, even though it's not the Olympics.

> I'm a *disaster* at teaching science. No, that's not exactly true. I'm not getting through to a few pupils like Adam and Kirsty, but some of them understand. Jodie and Mark ask some useful questions and most of the others are interested to find out more. It just feels like I'm a disaster. My explanation of water displacement and density needs a good deal of rethinking, but last week when we did an experiment on how materials change we got some really interesting results. We've even had time to display written work on the wall. I'd like to have all my class interested and the truth is that can happen sometimes. Just because a few of them didn't understand displacement and density this time, it doesn't cancel out the other successful lessons we've had. It's not realistic to think I can make science lessons work for everybody all of the time. There's been a problem in my plans lately and I'll try to put that right in the revision session in a couple of weeks' time. There's a good chance that one more explanation is all they need.

Searching for contrary evidence is an antidote to any natural tendency we may have to filter out positive details in favour of negative generalisation. The search needs to be genuine, and not such an intellectual quest that it leads to 'paralysis by analysis'. The aim is to move forward and do something constructive. Otherwise we or our pupils will endlessly indulge our analytical self-talk instead of taking action. Self-effacing, negative personal put-downs may protect self-esteem from attack, but disputing our rush to negative criticism can be healthier once the temporary pay-off of negativity is abandoned.

Reframing negative perceptions more positively

Disputing evidence can in itself lead to a positive reframe or switch of focus. Success in this can lead individuals to stop rating themselves and perceive adversity as annoying rather than catastrophic. Like changing a picture frame, we change the effect the statement has by putting it in a different, more realistic and positive context. It is easy to be cynical about this and think it is taking a Pollyanna, rose-tinted view of the world. That is clearly to underestimate the human capacity to be upset by events and take a blacker than necessary view of them. Whenever, in response to a frustrated negative comment, we say, 'No, that's not exactly true . . . ' we are inviting a more positive reframe. We marshal several pieces of evidence to dispute distorted thinking and this changes what we originally believed. Lindenfield (1995) sees considerable skill in using reframed statements as opening comments, which is a more direct way to use reframing.

Statement: I'm afraid this report is on the short side.
Reframe: You'll be pleased to hear this report is concise and to the point.

Statement: This is a scruffy piece of handwriting.
Reframe: I can read this, but I find it hard to make out some of the letters. We'll need to look again at that.

Statement: I got at least six answers wrong out of ten.
Reframe: Four answers right. I'm getting something right.

Statement: So much still to plan, it's a nightmare.
Reframe: I've already started planning. We'll see what happens.

Statement: Don't talk when I'm talking.
Reframe: I can teach better when you're listening, thanks.

Statement: I turned in my written work late.
Reframe: I finished my written work, even if it was a bit late.

Reframing can also be a response to global criticism from the adult inside a child's head.

Statement: You're *slow!*
Reframe: Just because I'm a slow thinker, it doesn't mean that I'm a *poor* thinker.

Statement: You're *always* behind the others.

Reframe: I'm often behind the others, but that doesn't mean that I'm *always* behind, or that I'm no good. Sometimes I take longer and still do good things.

A test of how deeply ingrained is our use of 'should' or 'must' can easily be made. Try taking each of the statements such as 'I'm slow', or 'I'm untidy' and devising a 'should', such as 'I *should* be able to do this quickly' or 'I *should* be tidy'. I have tried this with a group of trainee teachers and they completed the task without much difficulty.

One of the most charitable reframes of parental violence I know comes from Monty Roberts, who found a less painful way to break horses to a saddle than that of his father. Instead of tying the horse with ropes and dominating by force, Roberts learned how to persuade by signals and body language. In this example, we have a compassionate reframe of his relationship with his father.

> I broke horses by whispering to them. . . . If that was right, then it destroyed my father's life because all the things he had done before that were *wrong*. And he couldn't handle it, and when I looked up at him he had his mouth open and his first words were 'What the hell am I raising here?' And I didn't expect that . . . he took a piece of chain and beat me till I was in the hospital. Oh sure, I resented him for it. If someone is grossly unfair to you and physically abusive to you, you ought to resent it. But I don't hate my father. I don't hate him. If it wasn't for my father's really tough handling of horses, I probably would never have been dedicated enough to do what I'm doing. So in a way, he did me a great favour by swinging the pendulum so far towards pain and restraint that he caused me to have to find a better way . . . other people have broken horses by violent means and, yes, the horses were gentle and did their job. But they didn't do it as well as when they wanted to.
>
> (Monty Roberts, 'QED', BBC Television, July 1997)

Most reframing that concerns us in the classroom is not so emotionally complex as this. I have found that feedback on tasks, ways of presenting ideas to children and classroom dialogue can involve disputation of global beliefs and labels. Useful disputational questions (after recognising how pupils feel) are:

Why is it so awful that . . . ?

How is it really terrible that . . . ?

What is being exaggerated here?

What is still OK?

What's meant by *everything*?

How often really is *always*?

Learning a practical strategy to enhance this

Ellis and Seligman describe a practical strategy as easy to remember as ABC. Seligman suggests that if 'A' is for adversity, something that goes wrong, the event or situation, then 'C' stands for its consequences, how we feel and what we do. The point to grasp is that 'A' (adversity) does not actually cause 'C' (consequences) but actually depends on 'B', our beliefs. An example would be that if the adversity were that we broke a vase, the reaction we experienced (consequences) would depend on what we already believed about breaking that particular vase. If we believed the vase was valuable, the consequences would be different from breaking a vase that was believed to be almost worthless. Although this seems simple enough, it works for every reaction we have, even the more obscure ones. We do not always recognise this because there are so many subtleties within our spectrum of beliefs. If there were no truth in this, individuals would respond exactly the same way. They do not. An example of the ABC structure concerning a pupil would be:

Adversity: My best friend, Sarah, got picked instead of me for the singing part in the school play.

Beliefs: The teacher, Mrs Jackson, has never liked me and Sarah is one of her favourites. No wonder I didn't get picked.

Consequences: I just went all silent because I wanted to cry, but didn't want the others in the class to see me. Then I felt angry about being left out.

Ellis and Seligman realised that it is not possible to change the adversity once it has taken place. Disputing the negative belief, proposed Ellis and Seligman, means that more positive feelings and actions (consequences) follow. In the case of this pupil, her negative beliefs to be disputed could include:

Beliefs: My singing voice is no good and everybody thinks I can't remember my lines.

Beliefs: It shouldn't be like this! I can't stand it! I'd like to get my own back! I'm worthless.

As beliefs vary so much from one person to another, the disputation needs to be personal too. A teacher can help only so much by disputing a child's belief. The real prize is to have taught a pupil how to dispute their own unfounded belief. Disputing on behalf of a pupil is counter-productive because their belief is what counts. We can influence beliefs but it requires the pupil themselves to change. Put this sequence together and we have an ABCD of learned optimism: A – adversity; B – belief; C – consequences; and D – disputation.

Adversity (pupil):	I got all these sums wrong.
Belief:	Everybody seems to understand except me. I'm hopeless at maths.
Consequences:	I felt so miserable all I wanted to do was run home. I don't want to do any more maths because it makes me feel stupid.
Disputation:	Even if I couldn't do this part of my maths, it doesn't mean I'm totally stupid. I understand some of it. It's hard, and Darren, Claire and Michael don't understand either.

Adversity (pupil):	Sophie wouldn't play with me today.
Belief:	Sophie likes Rachel better than me.
Consequences:	I felt lonely and upset. I hated Sophie and Rachel for leaving me out.
Disputation:	Sophie can't play all the time. I don't know that she likes Rachel better because people can have lots of friends and you don't have to have favourites.

Adversity (teacher):	I got criticised by the headteacher for arguing with a mother who turned up after school to discuss her child's progress.
Belief:	I'm always too argumentative and can never say the right thing. Parents shouldn't try to do my job for me, and the head should give me more support.
Consequences:	I walked out of the school as soon as I could. I spent the rest of the evening feeling angry and upset. I felt like shouting and phoned my best friend for a good old moan.
Disputation:	I really did argue with a parent; no denying that. Maybe she was pretty stressed herself and my brooding about it won't change anything. She's been understanding in the past and we've got on well. The head is usually supportive and I'm probably exaggerating things.

The difficult part is to identify what belief is driving the emotional consequences. This is why catching ourselves automatically using global labels and exaggerations is such a helpful starting point. Labels can point to a deeply held negative belief, which we may then learn to identify.

Suppose the reality is that it really is terrible, awful and depressing. Some events in life are difficult to dispute, like the loss of a loved one or the end of a close relationship. Surely, we strongly need to validate our feelings of sadness and despair? Even brooding and the depths of despair have their limitations. Seligman suggests that as soon as we dispute the *usefulness* of hanging on to the misery we can actually feel better. Disputing the usefulness of brooding is his way of sidelining the negative thinking, by leaving it, going out and doing something else. In negative thinking, such as brooding, there is likely to be thought and feeling, but no real action. Action is needed to complete the trio of thought, feeling and action, without which it is difficult to be distracted from a negative focus.

The effect of disputing exaggerated or distorted beliefs is a positive 'E' for 'energised'. This is Seligman's term, though 'E' for 'effect' is also used by others. Easy though the ABCD acronym is to remember, it requires effort to put it into practice and we may frequently forget this is necessary. Dryden (1996) comments that disputing negative beliefs may feel 'all wrong' as we try to internalise an approach which makes perfect sense, but is not yet fully believed. The gap between how we feel and what we dispute is very real indeed and it takes time to catch up. This point is taken up with more detailed examples in Chapter 8.

Teaching pupils to do the same

It would be strange to find a classroom where there is a positive atmosphere, run by a negative, disparaging teacher. I have never found one. A strong influence of attitudes in any classroom is likely to be the teacher, which is why understanding an ABC strategy as a teacher (though not *perfect* understanding) comes before teaching children to do so for themselves. Seligman believes that we can teach the ABC framework to pupils as young as 7. Seeing the connection between adversity, belief and consequences is a crucial step (Seligman 1990: 236). The main point to get across to children is that how we feel does not suddenly come from nowhere. It comes largely from what we already believe about events or our situation in them. Disputation can be learned.

> Disputing and reframing are cognitive skills. Children can learn that skill at a very young age. They can learn to have self-affirming statements like, 'I can put my hand up without calling out', 'Yeah, this work is hard, but when I do my plan, when I do these three things it's still hard, but not *so* hard to get my writing done.' Kids will say 'I've got no friends. *Nobody* cares about me.' And you say 'Well what about Michael?' and then we get into the useful dispute about *nobody*. Some children grow up with a negative explanatory style, and if it's not challenged, they will grow up more stressed than other people. Cognitive reframing is also an important aspect of teacher-training, because we're all going to get stressed at some point, but we won't be as stressed so often if we can look again at this process of reframing.
>
> (Bill Rogers, interview, 1997)

This contrasts with 'being positive' with children while not acknowledging the reality of their situation.

Suppose they were ill and missed a school trip. It's no good saying 'The chances are there's another trip soon. Look on the bright side and don't worry.' If you say that, it's rather like saying 'You lost one leg, so hop about on the other one and you'll be fine.' You have to acknowledge how they feel and let them know they were heard. Only they themselves can rethink. You can help, but you can't do it for them.

(Primary-school teacher)

Teaching children to be positive about setbacks involves exploring the well-tried ABC model with them. We can do this by talking through an example such as the two given earlier in this chapter concerning maths and children playing together. Seligman clearly states that children need to learn that a thought has always triggered the negative feelings they have. If children can learn to find that thought, they can dispute it.

In teaching children to learn optimism, a challenge for a creative teacher (and there are many of these in the profession) is to practise the tasks in the Learned Optimism checklist.

Learned Optimism checklist

1   Teach children that how we feel does not usually come from nowhere. It comes from what we already believe about events, or our situation.
2   Talk them through the ABCD strategy, using examples.
3   Teach them that a *thought* has triggered negative feelings they have. If children learn to find that thought, they can dispute it.
4   Teach them to dispute *always*, *never*, *everything* and other global permanent labels.
5   Teach them to dispute unhealthy *shoulds* and turn them into preferences.
6   Teach them that we frequently forget to do all this.

These six tasks can be attempted within day-to-day learning, or by setting up a number of supportive group sessions looking at these issues as study-skills. My preference is for as much as possible to be done moment by moment on a daily basis so that positive teaching and learning are not something turned on and off like a tap. The attraction of working with pupils during a group session, set up for the purpose, is that focused discussion is possible. The ABCD strategy, for example, needs to have time set aside to discuss and develop it, so a group session such as 'circle time' can be useful for this.

KEY POINTS

- Wasted emotion can result from what I will call 'reminiscence fantasy'. This focuses on an imagined ideal outcome unrelated to what actually happened.
- *Always, never, everyone, nobody* are clues identifying the distortion of over-generalisation. They close the doors of possibility because they label in too wide a way for there to be any detailed information.
- *Brainy, stupid* or *failure* are similarly global labels which carry too little detailed information.
- *Shoulds, musts* and *oughts* can be changed to healthier preferences.
- *'I prefer'* statements allow us to take some responsibility for our feelings.
- Preferences may need to be stated so as not to imply *shoulds*.
- The ultimate inflexibility would be to say that we *should not* use the word 'should'. The effort of avoiding all *shoulds* is frankly not worth the anxiety.
- Key statements to use in disputing for ourselves are to say 'No, that's not true because . . . ' or 'I'm off track in thinking that because . . . '.
- Key questions are: 'What's missing that would describe some parts as more successful?' and 'What is still OK?'
- Remember the ABCDE? Of these, B and D are the important ones.
- Beware 'paralysis by analysis'.
- We will frequently forget all this.

Chapter 3

Learning lessons from teachers

She concentrates on talking about things that children can do. She talks with them about their interests. There are small tasks with rewards, and she is consistent about things. There is trust and warmth with praise for little things.

(First-school headteacher)

Reframing instead of negative self-rating

Positive personal qualities, such as trust, warmth of personality and un-conditional regard for pupils, cannot simply be learned from a book. I have in mind the adage, 'For every complex problem there is a simple solution, and that solution is wrong.' We cannot copy a teacher's qualities of unconditional regard for pupils, any more than we can exhibit warmth if we do not feel it. We can emulate, but not copy, good management of children's behaviour. Copying another's ability and achievement so that we can feel positive and worthwhile is irrational. A more reasonable ambition would be to learn something from teachers who are trying out techniques of reframing.

In this chapter I have included classroom examples based on the ideas in Chapter 2. There are examples of learning to reframe and minimise unhealthy self-rating. There are practical ideas for teaching children to dispute commonly held, but unreasonable views of success and failure. I have also included examples of how teachers try to improve relationships with their pupils.

Adapting what Albert Ellis (1962) said, teachers and pupils do not have to achieve in all possible respects in order to consider themselves worthwhile. Trying to be successful is sane enough, but strong drives for achievement, if strongly associated with self-worth, are known to lead to stress (Ellis 1962: 63). The nub of the problem for many pupils and teachers lies in flawed thinking about comparisons, particularly comparisons in relation to the achievement of others. The message of this and other chapters is that certain kinds of comparison can lead to self-rating and therefore to unnecessary stress. How does this come about?

Comparisons of performance, such as how well we did compared with last time, are valid, and necessary in education. Classrooms are places where assessment is an expected part of daily learning. Stress does not come from assessing a particular performance, but from beliefs about its lasting significance. Comparisons are flawed if they illogically transform fragments of performance into more enduring self-ratings. There are plenty of examples. Towards the end of the 1990s many UK teachers saw school rated against school, and teacher against teacher under a broad principle of competition for improvement. Some of the most hard-working teachers I knew at the time believed that adverse criticisms were personally aimed at them. In some cases school inspectors rated teachers' performances after observing their lessons. Logically we might know that such negative comparisons between our own and others' achievements are destructive, but as teachers we already make comparisons as part of the job. Here lies the grand illusion of comparison between snapshots of quite different activities, different schools and unique individuals. Making comparisons has an obvious familiarity for teachers. It is difficult to emphasise the importance of achievement in education without making comparisons against known expectations. Unfortunately, it is a small but illogical step from that to attaching comparisons of 'self' and 'other' worth on the basis of a recent performance. The cul-de-sac down which we have just walked is called 'self-rating'.

The flaw in self-rating is to have transformed a moment of success or failure into something else. A reasonable aspiration is to be a good teacher and to try to improve what we do. Understandably this can lead to looking around for role models and forming an opinion of what we understand as good and bad. A professional understanding of 'educational standards' helps to reinforce this. Not all teachers think this way, but if we are ensnared into making frequent personal comparisons of self-worth against another (even imaginary) capable individual, a well-known trait emerges. The tendency is to ignore any positive qualities we might already have in the perfectionist search for those that we think are still missing. This may even be something that happens subconsciously. We focus on a negative detail taken out of context, ignoring the other more positive features and conceptualising the whole experience on the basis of a fragment (Bernard and Joyce 1984: 69).

Locked into this thinking trap we can acquire enormous fears of taking chances, of making mistakes and failing at certain tasks. This fear tends to sabotage the very achievement we want (Ellis 1962: 64). It is senseless to equate individual achievement with personal worth, since we have no control over the achievement of others. The individual who must always succeed in an outstanding way, says Ellis, is 'fighting to best others'. He points out that making comparisons of worth is other-directed, rather than self-directed. The result can be to set impossible personal tasks and goals to achieve. An act of comparison as a person can consequently be an act of self-rejection if the comparison is unfavourable.

Knowing this, and even agreeing with it, may make no difference. Logically, an antidote would be to abandon ratings of self-worth. I do not think this is as easy as it sounds. As Bernard and Joyce (1984) put it, aspiring teachers take far too much notice of someone else's opinion of a teacher, or of themselves as a teacher. A fairly common response, in my experience, is for a teacher to understand the folly of making comparisons. The teacher will say, 'Yes, I know all that', but still hang on to negative judgements of self-worth because of the strong feelings which accompany them. Suppose, for example, another teacher is better than we are at using a computer or better at teaching mathematics. That is a reality. It is not an indicator of personal worth unless we have chosen it to be. As a comparison it can raise a negative response such as saying 'I feel really useless about not being able to use a computer as well as so and so can.' Unless this is put into perspective, the feeling of uselessness *becomes* the explanation, such as 'I feel useless, therefore I *must* be a useless (unworthy) person.' The feeling itself does not lie. It really does matter to me that I feel useless using this computer, and in the immediate emotional moment 'I feel useless' translates to 'I am useless'.

Negative thoughts and feelings can have a strongly debilitating effect. As research by David Cannon of the London Business School suggests, feedback on successes and failures is not seen as being balanced even when there seems to be an equal amount of praise and criticism. 'The oar of negative feedback has disproportionate weight, threatening to steer one in circles' (Gillies 1997). A more positive classroom script, or one that might be used with a pupil, goes something like this:

> Just because you feel *useless* at doing this, it doesn't mean you are. The feeling is very real, isn't it? But it's not helping much if you turn the strong feeling you have into the *explanation*. You've connected two things that are not the same. You feel bad, but that doesn't mean you *are* bad. There's a real temptation to say everything must be useless because you had some difficulties and it made you feel useless. It might be that you just take longer, or maybe you need a bit more practice this time. I know you get worried because other people understand more quickly, but it's only quicker, not necessarily better. Sometimes it might be better, but it isn't always like that. Give yourself a chance by taking a bit longer to get there.

In the short term, we can try to stop for a second to notice the automatic connection individuals make between the strong feelings they have and negative labels they use. Teaching children to do this is a much more challenging but not impossible task. In the longer term, we can actually prove to ourselves that labels such as 'useless' are self-defeating. The acid test is to observe over time how inaccurate labelling, often made as a result of irrational comparisons, makes the emotional state worse and actually prolongs negative feelings. Any initial response to adverse events may change little, but with practice what we do and how we feel as a consequence could become very different indeed. Dryden (1996) makes the point that intellectual understanding about labels, irrational beliefs, 'shoulds', 'musts' and thought-traps is not enough in itself. It is important to dispute these labels with some strength and emotion or nothing happens to change things. Initially the steps we take to reframe will be small ones requiring further practice. New and different approaches can feel strange until they are practised, rather like some of the awkward physical positions practised in sports, or those needed to learn the violin. They seem strange, but after a while they curiously feel right.

> Craig sprays his own and nearby children's work with ink from the pens he sucks. If there is disruption it will be down to Craig. Let's put it this way. Craig and I have certainly had our moments. He invites the worst of my thoughts and is almost guaranteed to be inattentive and the centre of attention. I set the class a writing task which included a quality target of accuracy in copying some details from a printed sheet. My stress levels can rocket when I see Craig has some way-off spellings, because they're things he already knows about. The automatic thoughts I had, when I looked at his work today, were 'Don't you ever listen? I might have guessed you would . . .'. I could feel my stress level rising. These thoughts surfaced fast, but I noticed that Craig had obscured his worksheet with his writing hand – he's left-handed, yet had managed to get words in the right order. Checking myself to reframe, I said 'Craig. You're able to put those words in the right order. Well done! Now let's just move that worksheet so you can see to copy accurately. Look at the spellings again and you'll make a really good job of that.' I saw him visibly relax and glow a little, but the effect on me was even more positive. I felt very pleased with myself for turning round the situation from negative to positive, remembering to catch those thoughts.
>
> (Primary-school teacher)

The next day I saw this teacher and asked her if she had any new reframing story to tell. 'No', she said honestly, 'I completely forgot to reframe.' At first, the practice of reframing will be characterised by forgetting and not having the emotional energy to reframe. As an antidote to self-rating, reframing is worth practising, but not worth the worry about temporarily forgetting. After a subsequent brush with difficult children she told me about the following reframe, this time outside the lesson, reframing through later reflection.

> English, year 7, last two periods on a Wednesday. I'm struggling with this class so I opted to do drama. It certainly was drama. They were rowdy, rude and disruptive, completely thrown by the task and the classroom assistant looked on in pitying fashion as I battled on. Afterwards, I mentioned to a colleague what a disaster it had been, but then I began to reflect a bit. There had been ten or fifteen minutes' discussion about their earliest memories and that had really grabbed their attention. I think that every pupil contributed

and they mostly listened to each other. Their drama performances *were* watched by each other with interest, and there was enthusiasm. During the session, all I could think of was what was going wrong. I guess afterwards I reframed the experience and, rather surprisingly, I really felt better about the whole thing. I could look my colleague in the eye and say 'I'm getting there!'

Critics of reframing could argue that the strategy puts an unrealistically positive view on failure and error. I disagree, because this would be to assume reframing is about 'being-positive-at-all-costs'. Positive thinking as reframing is not a rule-bound 'should', or an inflexible 'always be positive!' Reframing is a way of moving forward, trying to recognise some of the underlying feelings, and making the best of failures. The uncritical positive thinker is one who always looks on the bright side of life and always rushes to reframe (note the unreasonable demands of an 'always'). There is no need to pretend that the boat has not capsized when it has. We deny reality when we cannot face it, such as in serious personal loss, shock and grieving. A closer examination of the teacher's drama lesson shows that she accepted that year 7 were rowdy, rude and disruptive, thrown by the task, and that the classroom assistant looked on in pitying fashion. She could have gone into the staffroom and exchanged problem stories with a colleague, thereby inviting similar stories. She could have blamed the children, the weather or the school policy for behaviour. There is something to be said for sharing difficulties, so long as this does not reinforce a generalised label of 'terrible'. Rathbone and Benedict (1980) describe how staffroom moaning is not without its problems. 'A teachers' staffroom talk can cause you to get more burned out because you just talk about your nagging problems and they just talk about their nagging problems, and it's just going to get worse and get both of you convinced that everything's terrible.'

The basis of much effective classroom reframing is what Seligman (1990) calls 'de-catastrophising' negative perceptions. The labels of 'awful' and 'terrible' are expressions of frustration at things not being the way we would like them to be. A teacher's approach to de-catastrophising children's use of the global word 'awful' is described:

> I thought I was being positive and I asked Sarah, who's aged 11, what she would most like to be helped with. 'I just wish', she said, 'that I wasn't so *awful* at maths.' Actually, I got the reframing wrong this time and said, 'If you keep telling yourself you're awful Sarah, you'll never really improve. You *have* to stop calling yourself *awful*.' I caught myself using a 'never' and a 'must' or a 'should' disguised as a 'have to'. I won't say this was a tragedy because we have a good relationship, but on reflection I really could have teased out that word 'awful' and ended on a more positive note. Telling Sarah to stop calling herself 'awful' could just make her feel, 'Well, here's something else I'm not doing right!' I could more usefully have said, 'There's not really enough information for me to help when you say that it's awful,

Sarah. I need to know a bit more.' I could then have asked her, 'If it's that word "awful" you're using that's the problem, which bits of maths are the worst, and which bits are less awful?' She might reply 'Everything's awful', but I would still try to tease out the information. I might even say, 'It might feel that way, but I'm trying to find some smarter explanation for this than *awful*.' That might give me the chance to talk about the small bits of progress, the specific things Sarah *can* do and we could find the next steps she might take. It's important to talk about the steps she gets right and look for the chances to reward and encourage those. My approach would be to narrow down those parts of maths that Sarah found hard, be realistic about them, and get her to see some of her progress.

(Primary-school teacher)

This teacher gently challenged Sarah's global label. In the heat of the moment, reframing opportunities can be lost, but rarely are they lost for ever. Part of learning to reframe is to reflect and run the video-recording of the mind again, in readiness for noticing some future opportunity to reframe. Processes of change depend on awareness and action. We have little conscious control over what we might notice, but we can become predisposed to look for chances to reframe.

Strategies to turn awareness into action

A long-recognised difficulty, described over twenty years ago, is 'how to get the gut to accept what the brain knows is true' (Maultsby 1977: 89). Putting intellectual insights into practice means adjusting to new thoughts. Many of these will seem illogical compared with the old, not-extinguished emotional feelings. They will most probably not feel right. The gap between emotions attached to old thoughts and new insights is sometimes very uncomfortable until action proves differently. Action is the engine of change. Action, which means actually trying out ideas, is central to proving for ourselves that they work, and several practical steps can help here. I want to emphasise that the process of closing the gap between initial awareness and taking action is likely to be a remarkably slow one. It is slow, partly because there are other tasks in a teacher's day, and slow because we are only human and it takes time to act, adjust and change. Even if we want to take a positive view of events there is no guarantee that we will be able to do this every time.

A first practical step is to become aware of not over-reacting to pupils' negative global judgements. The vast majority of these (I'm *awful* at maths, swimming, computing, cooking; this is a *terrible, bad, hopeless* piece of work) are self-protective comments. This does not mean they are unimportant, even if they seem to be laughed off with black humour. They carry with them very real feelings and beliefs, but are understandable as being allowable self-protective comments. We all make self-protective comments. Often they are announced in advance (I'm sorry this meal/cake/report/essay is such a complete disaster).

In reality, it is not bad, good or unusual for anyone in the world to use self-protective comments. I do not think for one minute that knowing about self-protective comments will stop us using them. They reduce the element of threat in situations where self-esteem could be eroded.

Trying anything new can be threatening, as can most things involving a degree of skill or confidence. Public speaking or solo musical performances are obvious examples, but the classroom is a peculiar place. It is where on a daily basis there are bound to be new things to learn. A consequence of achieving success is often to be given something even harder to do and pupils' protective comments are an understandable response. If we over-react to dispute their claims of inadequacy, simply agree with them (yes, it *is* a terrible piece of work) or deny them (don't be so silly – it's really not terrible) we can easily be drawn into the protective personal drama of their frustration. If it feels terrible, then in their eyes it probably is. Until evidence gently shows them otherwise, there is a strong chance that self-rating will take over, and they may confirm their most negative but illogical labels of failure.

Perfection concerning reframing says, 'This *should* work every time, I *should* remember to do this every time, and I *should* remember the right words to say in the classroom.' The reality is rather like knowing it is a good thing to hold open doors for other people. There are days when we just let them swing back as we go through. If the gut is to accept what the brain knows is true there will be near-misses, lost opportunities and forgetfulness along the way.

Tuning in to how pupils feel

Classroom reframing tries to turn labels of self-worth into less permanent but more positive perceptions. Not everyone is immediately ready to reframe, however, even if they know how. Gray (1992) mentions the importance of reaching the trough of a wave of discontent without someone coming along too soon to try to fix it. People have a right to feel upset. Disputing what pupils say is not a very effective first step because what they say is a clue to how they feel and they most probably need those feelings validated. Disputing is a second step. First, we need to acknowledge pupils' frustration by finding the words to recognise with them that feeling *awful* is real for them. We do not need to agree with the substance of their protective statement, that what they say is actually true, but we do need to recognise their frustration.

> The trouble with agreeing with a child that something actually *is* awful or a disaster is that it is easy to get sucked into the emotional tangle. You want to agree and empathise a bit, but sometimes it can feel as if it means your teaching wasn't clear enough or that a pupil *should* have got it by now, or is whingeing yet again. Maybe you feel that by now they ought to be able to cope without falling apart. It all depends on how strongly you feel these things yourself as a teacher. I've found that no matter what happens, the first

need a pupil has is to feel that you understand their feelings of inadequacy. You can't move on to practical solutions unless you've at least partially agreed and said something like 'Well maybe you do feel like that, but that doesn't mean you . . . ' or you could take a little more time to tease out what the *awfulising* actually means. It's tempting to go straight to a solution or sweep aside the problem because of the feelings you have yourself as a teacher. But they need to know you understand their difficulties, don't they? They need to know their feelings are real.

(Middle-school teacher)

Briefly empathising with an individual by partially agreeing is so often missed out. A practical goal can be much more attractive if it seems to offer a quick way of solving difficulties. (Gray (1992: 37) argues convincingly that men are far more likely to play a premature 'Mr Fixit' role than are women.) The teacher in the example quoted earlier recognised the pupil's difficulty by saying, 'Well maybe you feel like that.' She then disputed the pupil's view of things by saying 'but that doesn't mean . . . '. She did not try to change negative thoughts for unrealistic positive ones to concrete over the difficulties. Nor did she deny the pupil's feelings. That would be like the denial of parent to child saying, 'Your knee doesn't hurt. Stop making such a fuss, it's only a scratch.' It plainly does hurt at the time. Sometimes it is possible to use the actual words a pupil has said and turn them around, signalling partial agreement.

I can understand when you say you're too tired and bored to do this. Maybe you are. Some of it *can* be tiring and this is not really how anyone wants to feel. You probably have hopes for it to be different, but feeling you have no energy doesn't mean it will *stay* like that. Feeling bored doesn't mean you're no good at it. Feeling bored doesn't mean it is not useful to try again.

So far I have outlined a strategy in which we try not to over-react and we acknowledge frustration. We are clear about the reality of the situation, then we help pupils to dispute irrational global labels. The strategy I have suggested is not an *always*-do-this rule. Teachers tend to work intuitively, so fixed rules are counter-productive. In any case, however good the strategy and language we use, the emotional content of the teacher's voice-tone overrides the most sympathetic of words. The language we use to acknowledge pupils' frustrations includes an appropriate tone of voice, posture, facial expression and other body language. The following examples could be spoken in a variety of ways, but a sympathetic adult tone is intended rather than an aggressive, sarcastic or complaining emotion in the sound. So much is carried by voice-tone, eye-contact and body language that these examples can only be a guide.

I think it *is* hard to do . . . but that doesn't mean. . . .

It sounds as if you're finding that hard . . . had you thought about . . . ?

> I know you said you're useless, so I guess you must *feel* like that. . . .
>
> This is really difficult and frustrating isn't it, maybe we need to . . .
>
> That must be so frustrating . . . let's see if there's another way.
>
> That's a real disappointment . . . I wonder if. . . .
>
> I like the fact you're trying even though I can see you're not really enjoying this yet. . . .

The most positive affirmation we can give anyone when we acknowledge their frustration is our fullest possible attention. If we want to reduce pupils' frustration, listening is positive in itself and allows some of that frustration to burn itself out. If this is truly active listening, it has dimensions familiar to adults. It will include responding, occasional clarifying and asking for updates of the previous day's concerns (McKay and Fanning 1992: 249). Time and class size are constraints here, but there are usually opportunities to listen if we make them. The chances are that some pupils already have a low tolerance of frustration and they need to feel important through being heard. It is very hard for teachers to cope with pupils whose anger and frustration quickly surface, and even harder to listen sympathetically and actively. Why is it like this for some children? Ellis (1977) puts forward the following explanation with its usual crop of 'should' and 'must' addictions. If he is right, he has synthesised several irrational thoughts commonly held by frustrated and angry individuals.

> When you feel furious, your basic view consists of the idea that whatever frustrates you should and ought not to exist, that it not only proves unfair, but this unfairness again *must* not prevail, that you can't stand frustration, and those who unduly balk and block you amount to almost vermin who, once again, *should not* act the way they indubitably do.
>
> (1977: 186)

A similar need to let a pupil ventilate feelings before moving to a solution operates for one school staff dealing with bullies.

> We've got this system for dealing with bullying. We get the bully to talk to the member of staff least likely to be hostile to that particular child, somebody they might like better than another teacher. If the bully really hates you, there is no way you can talk to them. You get the bully to talk to you about what happened and it's important at first to let them go on and on. What you often get is a stream of defence and endless justification for what they've been doing – how awful the other child has been, how unfair school is. You let them run on and the point at which you can interrupt the defence, and start to work on a solution, is when the bully actually makes good eye contact with you. However long it takes, you *have to wait* for that point

of eye contact or it won't work. Then you say something like 'I think we've got a problem here. What are we going to do about it?' When the child accused of bullying makes eye contact you can start to talk about the victim. 'So and so is having a very difficult time . . . what can we do to make their life a little less difficult?' And it's at that stage you can involve the bully in thinking how the victim might be feeling. You get them to come up with ideas that might make the victim's life easier. A very simple idea they might have might be no more than 'leaving the victim alone' or saying 'hello' to them every day. Beyond that we use a written script and a programme we follow up with the bully.

(Middle-school teacher)

Testing for chances to reframe

How can we influence things in a positive way? One way is to teach pupils to understand the difference between temporary, specific problems and those problems which they think are permanent and pervasive. An opportunity to try this can be through organising a classroom discussion that I call 'Everything Always or Something Specific'. Its aim is to teach children to look for evidence to dispute negative reasoning and reframe. They learn the difference between absolutes, such as 'everything'/'always' and specifics such as 'yesterday'/'once'. I have in mind a group of children taking turns to give their view and trying to learn how to reframe more positively. This might be part of 'circle time' when pupils know they are trying to think about how they solve difficulties. The following ideas assume that teachers subscribe to the belief that discussing social and moral issues with children is worthwhile.

* (E) stands for *Everything and always*.
  This is a chance to dispute global labels and flawed thinking.
  Reframing can result from describing specific and more positive evidence.

* (S) stands for *Something and specific*.
  This is a chance to reframe in terms of other occasions when it was not like this, or suggest future action.

Examples:

(S) I sometimes forget things I need for school.
(E) I always forget all my school things.
(E) I can never remember anything.
(S) I need to find a better way to remember my sports kit.

(S) Jason sometimes messes around instead of working.
(S) Jason needs to find better ways to help our group.
(E) Jason always wastes our time when we do things as a group.

(S) Lots of problems today. I need to find just one success to balance this.

(S) Three problems together this time. Phew!

(E) It starts OK, but it always goes wrong.

(E) I always get kept in at break because the teacher doesn't like me.

(S) I got kept in at break because I wasted time when we were writing.

(E) Other people never get kept in at break.

(S) I didn't get picked for the school team because I did not play well in the last two matches.

(E) I didn't get picked for the school team because I'm no good at sport.

(E) I didn't get picked for the school team because no one likes me.

(S) You are not sharing the paints fairly this lesson.

(E) You three are just selfish.

(S) You three can learn to share equipment today so we can all use it.

(E) You're untidy.

(E) I'm untidy.

(S) There's paper on the floor and things to put away.

(E) This room is a mess as usual.

(E) I got top marks, so I'm brilliant.

(E) He got top marks, so he's brilliant.

(E) He got top marks so I'm hopeless.

(E) I got top marks, so I'm good at this subject.

(S) I got top marks so I did well this time in the test.

(E) You never ask me and I've got my hand up all the time.

(S) I didn't have a chance to answer this lesson.

(E) I never get a turn on that.

Building on this previous discussion material, a number of other classroom activities are possible. Some of the following are based on work by Ellis (1962) and some are my own. The aim of these activities is to break down misconceptions and labels of failure. They can be thought of as tasks which may be used for discussion with pupils or as inservice discussion with teachers learning to reframe. All tasks mentioned here benefit from giving examples to children, based on current classroom events.

Circle-time tasks

- Dispute the belief that school/life *should* be fair *all* the time. Sometimes it is definitely not fair.
- Explain to pupils that demanding everything should always be fair can lead to being angry and wanting to give up. Invite examples.
- Discuss with pupils that it does not mean they are not coping if they need to ask for help. It does not mean they *are* coping if they do not need to ask for help.

- Discuss with pupils how feeling bad about something does not always mean it *is* bad.
- Explain that a person's mistakes do not change their good qualities. People are not bad because they make mistakes, frustrating though they might be for those around them.
- Explain and discuss with pupils that something they are saying to themselves about a situation can cause them to feel upset. It is more helpful to question their thoughts about things because there may be a better way to look at things.
- Discuss with pupils how being liked by *everybody* is impossible. Being liked by *someone* is possible.
- Discuss with pupils how we would prefer people to recognise, praise and approve of every good thing we do, but they do not always do that.
- Explain/discuss how blaming someone for doing something we disapprove of presumes they had total control over themselves. Such is not always the case.
- Explain that blaming someone else for our feeling unhappy is ridiculous.
- Explain how not being very good at some things at school does not mean we are no good at anything.

The approach a teacher uses to discuss these points is bound to be personal, but there are ways to elicit responses:

I wonder if when (such and such happens) . . .
Here the teacher describes a typical incident and uses examples, including drama, to make it as 'concrete' as possible.

I wonder if you've ever said things inside your head like . . .
Here the teacher talks aloud using the self-defeating, global labels, the 'shoulds' and 'musts', and goes on to describe a typical incident the self-defeating speech might relate to. A positive outcome of this approach would be to have introduced the terms 'self-defeating', or self-sabotaging, which may be entirely new concepts.

Suppose you kept on saying things like that? I wonder how you might feel if . . .
Here the teacher is beginning to dispute the value of self-defeating criticism.

Criticism and motivation

Mills (1997) has commented that most people unfortunately believe that self-esteem must in some way always be earned through accomplishments. Yet when self-esteem depends on accomplishments, it has to be earned repeatedly and is therefore not very secure. It is very difficult not to feel a better person by achieving something, doing something well like winning a tennis match or painting a picture that is admired. The trouble is that feeling a better person for having achieved, and basking in the warm glow of success as a *person*, leads to feeling much worse when things go wrong. The inappropriate grandiose positive feelings (about myself, instead of about the task I did) lead to inappropriate negative feelings about myself next time it goes wrong (Ellis 1998b).

The negative criticisms of others, even if well-motivated to help, are usually unwelcome. Here are four features of a positive classroom that a teacher may find helpful in supporting and maintaining pupils' self-esteem.

1 Absence of ridicule, sarcasm and comparison with other pupils.
2 Presence of encouragement and belief in the child's capacity.
3 Awareness that criticism of the individual is uninvited and unwelcome.
4 Separation of individual worth (something we have from birth to the grave) from rating of performance (variable, temporary and specific).

These four features are aspirations, rather than rule-driven demands. Compassion is probably needed to implement them, which could seem too saintly a requirement for an over-worked teacher. I mention compassion here because it is unfortunately misconstrued as a fixed character trait, something that either we have or we do not. It need not be a saintly characteristic. For some teachers it can be seen as far more than a trait and developed through understanding situations more fully. Compassion can be developed through better understanding oneself in relation to others and the events surrounding other people's lives (McKay and Fanning 1992: 84). Learned compassion, something we could acquire rather than a fixed trait, may seem bizarre, or 'not the real thing'. Such an idea as learned compassion could be swept aside without much difficulty because there is no proof that we can achieve it. If the possibility is taken on trust, some examples may help to explain its development.

One of the toughest tasks for any teacher is to improve a relationship with a pupil they do not like. Ultimately compassion hinges on an unswerving belief in children, however mistrustful of us they might be. Humphreys (1996), commenting on the child's mistrust, says, 'When you have lived in a world that has let you down frequently, you learn to be distrustful and a few expressions of unconditional regard are not going to lure you out of your defensive space.'

> I had this pupil Kirsty and I really did not like her. So I guessed pretty soon she didn't like me either. We had battles over her work and it was frustrating enough for me to become very critical and negative. I got sucked into arguments and she was resistant most of the time. I found it really difficult to find anything to praise, but by being more positive I discovered she *was* actually more likeable. I've done this with other children since. If you want them to be more likeable, really likeable, it's worth flogging on with some positive praise wherever you possibly can. They change a bit and so do you, and you really do like them in the end. As the old saying has it, 'You're going to catch more flies with honey than you ever will with vinegar.'
>
> (Teacher of 10-year-olds)

There is agreement in several cultures that compassion and tolerance of others begins with greater acceptance of oneself (Bernard 1986; Ellis 1962; McKay and Fanning 1992). I freely admit to knowing this, feeling it has a ring of truth, yet finding it immensely difficult at times to put into practice. The idea that accepting oneself comes before accepting others could focus the mind in a self-absorbed way. A more generous interpretation has been suggested by Ellis (1994), who talks about ways of working towards the goal of unconditional self-acceptance. According to Ellis, unconditional self-acceptance is knowing that we are fallible and realising that this state of affairs is far better accepted without condition. We accept in our gut that criticism and self-blame are misunderstandings of ourselves. Acceptance says that if people make mistakes, they are of course responsible for what they do, but not blameworthy as persons. The difference is between individuals rating their deeds and rating their global 'selves'. Instead of global self-rating they choose to accept themselves whether or not they perform well or are approved of by other people. They reframe their failures as feedback rather than as damnation (Ellis 1997a).

Unconditional self-acceptance means preferring to do well, but accepting that we very often do poorly, make mistakes, and are not especially competent. Accepting is never rating ourselves because of our mistakes or successes. The hard part is seeing that we never have to put ourselves down for failing at an important goal or being rejected by someone who we feel is important to us. *Conditional* self-acceptance is accepting ourselves when we do something well. *Unconditional* self-acceptance is accepting ourselves simply because we are human and alive. There need be no other reasons. Unconditional self-acceptance usually leads to less emotional anguish, and greater personal fulfilment. It does not eliminate sadness, loss and frustration, but it does eliminate needless anxiety, rage and depression. In Ellis's terms, through developing unconditional acceptance, anger turns to annoyance, anxiety becomes concern, shame becomes regret and depression becomes a more healthy sorrow.

Humphreys (1993) offers an antidote to criticism. He suggests teaching individuals that people really say more about themselves when they criticise, and through their actions, than they do about the person or thing they are criticising. He goes so far as to suggest that everything a person does or says is really a statement about themselves (1993: 100). Sometimes the statement is disguised, but often it is really an expression of a critic's own needs. That may be why it is sometimes not worth trying to persuade critics to admit they might be wrong. Their reasons for criticising are far removed from being right or wrong.

Unfortunately, criticism can be implied through the absence of praise from others. This may take the form of unreasonable self-talk, such as 'I did this and nothing was said about it so it must be a poor piece of work'. There are countless moments when teachers and pupils work hard without praise when they really need it. It is too easy to say that we all need praise as if it were our daily bread. People have their own concerns and these do not always include giving praise when it is deserved. Praise may be welcome, but absence of praise implies criticism only for some, not all individuals. Individuals vary in their need for the approval of others, and a few may continually seek approval. Absence of praise is therefore likely to have different effects on different pupils according to need. Praise, praise and yet more praise is important, but not a complete solution to coping with criticism because we can never be sure how it is received.

A positive classroom can be one where children and teachers have learned something about self-praise. (This theme is elaborated in Chapter 6.) Teachers, in my experience, are very good at praising children and rather less good at praising themselves. Low incidence of self-praise has long been known to contribute to poor self-esteem (Bernard 1990: 82). When we have done something well, we do not often pat ourselves on the back for a job well done. Yet we can kick ourselves mightily when we make mistakes. Up and down the country there are teachers who organise well and think nothing of doing so. They support colleagues, enthuse about personal teaching projects, yet still take their efforts for granted. Looking in the mirror, they still see mostly the negatives.

If the mirror could speak back, what might it say?

> You have to look for little things to praise yourself. The big projects take far too long for self-esteem to build and anyway you might spend your time worrying about the mistakes. Little things to praise yourself are what? Little things are not necessarily *small* things. 'I set a cracking pace in that lesson', 'I listened for longer than I wanted to a colleague', 'I organised the class name lists for the school trip', 'I was more patient with Darren, even though he irritates me', 'I remembered that Sue had a difficult day yesterday and I asked how she was', 'I complimented Rachel on the way she coped with the queue for drinks'. You see, for many people these things just don't count, do they? They only see praise as something bigger outside themselves, something other people give them if they do well. That way, they use someone else's opinion to value themselves, which is silly when you think about it.

KEY POINTS

- The process of closing the gap between insight and practice is likely to be slow and imperfect.
- If the gut is to accept what the brain knows is true there will be near-misses, lost opportunities for action and much forgetting.
- It is not bad, good or unusual for anyone in the world to use self-protective statements.
- Negative thoughts and feelings can have a disproportionate effect compared with an equal amount of praise.
- Inaccurate labels such as 'terrible' and 'disastrous' are self-defeating, make the emotional state worse and prolong the negative feelings for much longer than necessary.

- It is senseless to compare individual achievement in terms of personal worth, since we have no control over the achievement of others.
- An act of comparison is an act of self-rejection if the comparison is unfavourable about oneself.
- A pupil's mathematical 'awfulising' may not be effectively disputed without first recognising that that is how they really feel.
- 'Do your best' can be misinterpreted as 'Be the best'.
- Low self-praise contributes to poor self-esteem.
- Criticism can be implied through absence of praise.

Chapter 4

Strong expectations and pupil feedback

One of the strangest ideas, promoted partly by advertising, is that people are happiest when relaxing and doing nothing. I occasionally subscribe to this as being an antidote to stress, where there is an obvious benefit to be had. Most teachers welcome a holiday. Unfortunately, by this token, I could also believe that human happiness could ultimately be achieved through inertia and inaction. Several pupils in my classroom may have similar ideas about achieving greater happiness by doing absolutely nothing, a far cry from being persistent and tenacious. Happiness achieved through inertia and inaction has been described as an irrational idea (Bernard 1990; McWilliams and McWilliams 1991). We are happy when we are absorbed in human and creative pursuits, or when we are devoting ourselves to people or projects outside ourselves. John-Roger McWilliams and Peter McWilliams (1991) describe action as the necessary third side of a triangle of thought, feeling and action. Without action the triangle is incomplete and we are left ruminating and inattentive to creative possibility. There may be plenty of thought and feeling going on, but we are uninvolved unless we complete this with action. As a colleague recently put it, 'If you're not into *something* you're dead. Death is in the armchair.'

Moving from inertia to action requires effort that many pupils may not want to make. Learning to be tenacious and persistent sounds even harder. Tenacity is clinging on stubbornly in the face of difficulty and persistence is 'going the extra mile'. Creating classroom expectations about these is quite different from teaching pupils to know what the words mean. How do pupils force themselves to be tenacious and persistent? A number of pupils may expect that, because they want things to be done easily, without effort, there should be an easy way. They may think that everything they do must be as interesting and entertaining as television and video games. They may even expect that things will be done for them, or decide in advance that they are too stupid and incapable. The teacher can rarely know what expectations and attitudes children bring to the classroom, but these may be about entertainment and interest. To some extent teaching can of course be entertaining, and many of the best teachers I have observed are excellent presenters of their material. Even so, this is still an unrealistic expectation for children to have. Grumbles about learning being hard and boring imply that it should always be easy and interesting.

Having high academic expectations of pupils is not enough in itself to generate tenacity and persistence, but it is still important. High expectations of pupils regarding their level of achievement means what it always has done, pitching work at a challenging level. Most teachers would want to do this anyway, but some are very skilful in spelling out more clearly what is being aimed for. They see challenging work as important, purposeful and worthwhile despite the difficulties. They aim high and live with the difficulties of doing so. My hunch is that with some experience of teaching, high expectations can be transmitted to pupils in all sorts of little ways. These include skilful classroom language, gestures, pauses, humour, and considerable emphasis on the detail of what is important. These aspects of teaching are so interwoven that they tend to be habituated as part of a teacher's style. There are fortunately other skills and strategies that can be used to keep pupils involved. These are additional to giving strong emphasis to high academic expectations.

Four ways of generating more effective pupil involvement are suggested in this chapter. My aim is to focus on raising expectations, particularly about giving feedback. Expectations are rarely obvious in the classroom, and an outsider would find it difficult to know what habits of expectation are strongly established. The four ways are:

1   Promoting realistic classroom expectations.
2   Questioning without relying on volunteers.
3   Expecting feedback from pupil self-assessment.
4   Setting effective short-term deadlines.

Promoting realistic classroom expectations

Without necessarily liking it, maybe even greatly disliking it, pupils need to accept several realistic expectations about school life. These are uncomfortable realities, but understanding them is actually very positive. Teaching them to be realistic can help to emphasise that it is quite a negative attitude to expect that learning must always be enjoyable. Learning can of course be enjoyable, but not always enjoyable, because this suggests that responsibility lies solely with the teacher. If as a pupil I do not find learning enjoyable, and I think teachers definitely are there to make it so, I have a good excuse to drop out. Every inspiring teacher has their duller moments, and not every lesson can guarantee pupils' interest. Some lessons will inevitably deal with less interesting but still essential material. Teachers who try to transmit the idea that learning is 'fun and easy' do no favours to their pupils. There is no reward for failing at learning something which has already been described as 'fun and easy'. There is no reward in being bored having already expected to be interested.

Realities about hard work and effort are not very palatable for pupils. Some caution is therefore necessary when we face pupils with the reality of classroom life. Pupils are not going to take kindly to the nagging tones of a chastising parent. There seems to be a psychological switch inside their heads that recognises the emotional tones of nagging. Realities, however convincing, can lose impact if hearing them is resisted. One way to avoid this would be to turn the following statements into questions during a class discussion, allowing pupils to agree classroom realities for themselves. Another would be to pick a useful moment to reinforce them, using as sympathetic a voice-tone as possible. The ultimate aim would be to erode a number of unrealistic expectations concerning effort, work and achievement. Though very young children will require differently worded explanations from the following, the realities for pupils to understand are shown in the 'Classroom realities checklist' below.

Classroom realities checklist

- You can't always do things just because you like them.
- Things at school are not going to do themselves or be done for you (not very often).
- You need to learn that a benefit comes from doing them rather than putting them off.
- It is hard, but *not impossible*, to do them.
- If things are hard, that is the way they often are – hard.
- Sometimes things are boring.
- If things went wrong, they went wrong *this time*.
- You can't have everything you want.
- Refusing to give up in the face of difficulty can have positive outcomes.

I would not want to see any of these realities listed on a poster and displayed. Pupils need ownership of ideas, not simply to have them pasted to the wall as the school commandments. Realities are not what pupils usually want to hear, especially if the tone of teacher-voice signals that the relationship with pupils is far from warm. It is all too easy to sound like someone who thinks they know best, when ideally we want children to internalise these truths. Pupils can always deny and reject ideas if they want to, but handled sympathetically the seeds of change are often sown. It is worth remembering that pupils will protest most loudly just before they are ready to accept something they strongly resisted.

> Of course pupils don't want to hear that things won't magically do themselves! It's too obvious a statement to make isn't it? How can anybody be so stupid as to think I won't understand that things don't often happen as if by magic? It's just going to make me angry to hear that. But there's a jewel in the crown here and I can't see it for looking. If anything is magical, it's understanding that thinking things should be different, easy, finished by now, shouldn't happen, and so on really *is* self-defeating. We don't often want to accept what self-defeating habits can do. They WEAR YOU OUT!

So the magical short-term fantasy of wanting reality to be different is much more appealing. It can protect us from ourselves. But however hard we try, all that self-defeating beliefs will do in the end is defeat us because that's what they're destined to do. So the question is: 'Where's the self-defeating belief about easy and magical that pupils are hanging on to?'

(Rational-emotive therapist)

Expectations about tenacity and persistence are positive values, and we will need to sound positive whenever we encourage them. The most straightforward way to do this is to tell older pupils openly and frequently that tenacity and persistence are targets. Time and effort can be devoted quite openly in lessons to 'sticking it out' when the going gets difficult. Effort is certainly going to be needed to do this and be rewarded if possible. Much less straightforward, but still worth trying, is to boost expectations that tenacity and persistence are the norm. One of the secrets of doing this is to convince children that the teacher's tenacious, effort-filled agenda is actually theirs too. The proof of this can be discovered with younger children, even those aged 3. They can plan with a teacher what they do in the nursery themselves and spend sustained time doing it. Older children may be more suspicious about whether they have a choice, but the principle can still work. If individuals think there is a personal pay-off for effort, and some element of choice or ownership, they will often be very tenacious. Once the pay-off disappears, so may the tenacity.

We know from studies of children that persistence can be actively encouraged or discouraged. Claudia Mueller and Caroline Dweck of Columbia University undertook a research study that looked at the effects of two different approaches to giving praise. They found that children praised for intelligence actually did far less well and were less persistent than those who were praised for effort. This was a carefully detailed study which Mueller and Dweck describe in the *Journal of Personality and Social Psychology* (1998). They gave 412 children aged 10 years a task in which they performed well. Some children were then told, 'Wow that's a really good score, you must be really smart at this.' Others were told, 'Wow, that's a really good score, you must have worked really hard.' In subsequent tasks, the pupils rated for intelligence looked for tasks in which they were sure to do well. Those pupils praised for effort wanted the more challenging tasks where they could learn something. After a failure, children who had been told they were intelligent and clever (global ratings) displayed less persistence than those praised for working hard.

I mention this study because it coincides so closely with the view that rating personal worth is counter-productive (Ellis 1998b). A fixed personal high rating has to be continually re-achieved and sustained, which is logically impossible. A fragment of pupil performance does not lend itself to conclusions about ratings of intelligence, but it does lend itself to praise for effort. It is not surprising that pupils who were given the reason 'You must have worked really hard' wanted to persist. This is a value that is specific to the effort needed to do the task, not to a fixed notion of ability. It is 'of the moment', does not rate in a judgemental way, but instead praises performance as being the result of hard work done *this time*.

Questioning without relying on volunteers

Ways of keeping children involved, such as asking questions, inevitably involve pupils actively. The Greek philosophers knew this well, as Socratic questioning clearly exemplifies. Answering questions is all very well for those pupils who are keen to volunteer, but some children will still be able to coast along unless they are accountable. For all sorts of reasons, some children do not want to volunteer answers. They may be shy, reserved, content to let their friends do the thinking, resentful, threatened or lazy. The problem of teachers relying on volunteers has also been reported in small-group activities where some pupils progressively become uninvolved. They do not *expect* to be involved and therefore rely on their peers (Tuckman 1990: 296). Teachers counteract this as best they can, but several pupils in a class may easily be overlooked in the hope that somehow they will catch up. Shyness apart, this ignores how skilful certain pupils become at relying on others unless prodded into action. If questioning is a great teaching skill, then finding ways to encourage answers from everybody is even greater.

Imagine a scene regularly played out in classrooms. The teacher asks the pupils a question, such as 'Who can tell me the name of the nearest planet to the Earth?' and invites volunteers. There is a right answer to this question. Some pupils can be relied on to volunteer, while a small number of pupils rarely do so. The willingness of volunteers varies according to the nature of questions, but over a period of time a pattern emerges. Some pupils are habitually most likely to volunteer answers and others are unlikely to respond unless asked. There is nothing remarkable about this, except that habits can become deeply ingrained and accepted as the classroom norm. An alternative strategy is where a teacher targets pupils specifically as conscripts, turning the question around to something like 'Steven, see if you can tell us the name of the nearest planet to the Earth?', 'Rachel, do you think that's true?', 'What do you think, Simon?' The power relationship between teacher and conscript in these encounters is different from that of teacher and volunteer.

Using a child's name, and targeting them personally, is occasionally used to regain attention rather than gain it in the first place. For some children the coercion of being conscripted to answer could therefore be threatening, though my experience has been that it need not be. If it is established as a habit, pupils become more used to it if they realise it is not just to wake them up if they nod off. The interesting feature for me is how rare it is for teachers habitually to set out to use a style of questioning that targets individuals. This is understandable to some extent in order to maintain the flow of an explanation and reward more enthusiastic volunteers. Instead of a 'hands-up' directive to answer as volunteers, conscripting pupils is a 'hands-down' approach. One teacher who developed this simply sat down with his class and told them, 'For the next fifteen minutes,

I don't need hands up because I'll decide who to ask.' The effect was remarkable. Once pupils knew that anyone in the class was likely to be asked, they answered questions readily and were kept on their toes. A reasonable guess is that they were more likely to need to listen in the first place. There was an expectation of feedback being needed.

A helpful feature of the conscript style I have observed is the use of a 'person-centred' rather than 'teacher-centred' approach. In a person-centred approach, the aim is to ask 'What do *you* think, John?', 'Do *you* think that, David?' rather than 'What's the answer to . . . ?' Another teacher-centred example is 'Why did the Vikings invade Britain?' and a person-centred version is 'Why do *you* think the Vikings invaded Britain, David?' In teacher-centred questioning, the teacher might ask, 'What's the best way to go about working in groups?' In pupil-centred questioning, a teacher would ask, 'What do *you* think would mean that you had worked well in a group?' The aim is to gain as many personal responses as are useful, before going on to tease out the appropriateness of answers. In a teacher-centred approach there is sometimes a tendency to ask a question and partly answer it, or pose it in such a way that only one correct answer will do. Children learn all too quickly that if an adult asks the same question again, the answer was probably wrong. Adults usually stop asking the question once they are happy with the answer. In a person-centred approach, there are no clues, sometimes no praise, unless it is 'A really thoughtful answer, which helps us with the detail. Does anyone else have an answer?' Questions where more than one answer is possible are naturally going to lend themselves to this technique, but the idea is to involve pupils in thinking. Even if they never answer, all pupils can be 'ready to answer' as a result of raising expectations that they will.

It does not take much to deduce that expecting to have to respond is likely to prepare pupils differently. They are more likely to pay attention and think of something to say even before they are asked. An advantage, in my experience, is that occasional targeting frequently avoids the known problems of eager pupils dominating and shy, less eager or lazy pupils leaving answers to others. Conscription is effective, so long as it is not always, for everything and to the complete exclusion of enthusiastic volunteers. Volunteers may even be more forthcoming once it is established that every pupil is expected to answer as best they can. Much will depend on whether pupils see a question as a chance to learn or as a threat to self-esteem (Dweck 1986).

Expecting feedback from pupil self-assessment

The same principle can be applied to feedback from written work, notes and written comments. In a research project I undertook with two teachers, we further developed the need for pupil involvement using pupil self-assessment. Towards the end of 1996, two teachers in mid-career, along with me as a researcher, tried to put ideas about feedback from assessment into daily practice. I was not convinced that informal feedback was substantial enough to be called 'formative assessment'. The idea was to maximise pupils' involvement. We did this by increasing and strengthening their expectations that they would provide frequent written and spoken feedback. This came mainly from pupils making brief written self-assessments and informally reporting back to their teachers. Pupils, for example, when learning about electric circuits would know in advance that they were expected to report on their understanding of how to include a switch.

Over a period of time, our class of 10-year-old pupils increased their expectations about the need for feedback. We expected feedback during teaching sessions and later stretching over several days. The two teachers said that pupils' involvement and their focus on tasks increased. We suspected that increasing feedback during lessons could help in keeping pupils on track, minimise mis-understanding and signal areas in need of further explanation. However informal this was, the intention was to feed back into learning. Informally, teachers use formative assessment whenever they make a judgement about what to do next. As we were to discover, formative assessment is often taken for granted because it is an obvious part of informal feedback. Referring to formative assessment, Lidz (1991) summed up the problem for teachers and educators alike when faced with its familiarity: 'Assessment leading to improvement sounds so logical that practitioners often think that they already do it.'

We know that formative feedback is central to improving teaching and learning (Sadler 1989; Gipps and Murphy 1994; Black 1993; Black and Wiliam 1998). Without feedback as verbal exchanges, written responses, tests and assessments there is little firm basis on which to correct pupils' misunder-standings. If there is no feedback, there is little basis on which to steer their progress. Feedback implies action to be taken, even if it is not always followed up. Teachers already give feedback informally to pupils during lessons through their response to the various signals they pick up. They may, for example, self-correct during explanations in response to pupils' frowns of confusion. They respond during lessons to whatever pupils' comments, answers, and written and practical work there are. None of these responses is necessarily planned or strongly expected. Formative feedback is usually 'of the moment', or randomly accumu-lated, such as a growing pile of written assessments intended to be used later. We wanted to find out what would happen if feedback was more systematically planned for and frequently expected. An immediate objection to this might be that it is too time-consuming. In practice, this meant a change, rather than an increase to the teachers' workloads.

Rapid feedback can be very effective. In our research project we let pupils give feedback using brief 'help-slips' which they posted in a tin. This had a slot cut into the lid and pupils would write, 'In science I didn't understand about positive and negative wires.' We would ask for feedback part-way through a lesson, frequently enough for this to become an expectation. Teachers also created short self-assessment sheets for pupils to fill in. These are described in more detail in the next chapter, but consisted of a checklist of about six items. We found that the speed with which feedback is made available affected what action could be taken. The strength of pupils' expectation mattered, as did the usefulness of feedback generated. Not all feedback is useful or requires action.

Setting effective short-term deadlines

Pupil expectations, which I will call their *feedback expectancy*, can become habit reinforced through setting deadlines. The way this works is to build in frequent expectations that pupils will need to give feedback within a certain time. This can even be through a timed 'quality-control sheet' checked over a period of days. In some of the larger city stores, there are check sheets for cleanliness in public toilets, signed every hour by one of the workers. These simply indicate that something has been checked at a certain time. Older pupils can use checklists as a peer assessment where each pupil takes responsibility for others' checking (see below).

Quality checklist – story writing

PUPIL NAME: . . . .

Accuracy of information	by 15th
Spellings	by 17th
Punctuation	by 17th
Draft presentation	by 19th
Final copy	by 20th

Signed . . . .

A further example of *feedback expectancy* is to tell pupils in advance that they will be expected to discuss and write down findings and feed them back within a specified period of days. Expectations of feedback become implicit in numerous pupils' tasks once habits are established. A teacher might, for example, habitually expect feedback during an explanation or have already generated in pupils the expectation of feedback as a feature of the maths work they do. The strength of expectations can vary, depending on how demands for feedback were perceived and whether pupils were habitually involved in providing feedback. Examples of building a feedback habit include the teacher saying at an early stage:

> In about ten minutes, I'll expect you to be able to tell me . . . (implies that there is a deadline and feedback expected).

When you two return from the school library, you'll have about fifteen minutes before you show the rest of us what you found out . . . (implies a delayed deadline for presenting findings).

Friday morning first thing, I'll collect in your work on 'Conservation of the coastline' to look at and comment on . . . (implies feedback is a two-way process with a deadline).

Given that demands for feedback may arise both formally and informally, the strength of expectation can be said to vary. Expectations can therefore be declared strong or weak depending on a number of factors. 'Strong' feedback expectancy can be said to exist where there is no possible doubt that feedback will be required of pupils. The teacher generates feedback expectancy by involving all pupils at an early stage of a teaching session and setting a feedback deadline that is strictly kept. Feedback expectancy that is 'weak' is that to which only a few pupils bother to respond. It is infrequently demanded, promised then forgotten about, or has been built into a session far too late to have much effect.

Some features of strong and weak feedback expectancy can be identified and are listed in the box below.

Strong feedback expectancy

- Pupils are habitually targeted for feedback.
- Feedback is regarded as compulsory by pupils.
- Pupils are accountable.
- Feedback is demanded early in a session.
- Feedback is demanded early in a project.
- Deadlines are set for feedback.
- There is habitual discussion of feedback.
- Feedback is expected to lead to action.

Weak feedback expectancy

- Feedback is infrequently demanded.
- It is left up to pupils to volunteer feedback.
- Feedback is demanded too late to have much effect.
- Pupils are not accountable.
- Few or no deadlines are declared.
- There is little indication of feedback becoming habitual.
- Feedback is not followed up.

In strong feedback expectancy, pupils are accountable. Where feedback expectancy could be regarded as being much weaker, there is less accountability and only ever volunteers.

It's almost every teacher's experience, watching children 'tune out'. Some, of course, never really 'tune in' in the first place. I'm there teaching them French and it's a lesson full of questions and answers, repetition and involvement. You would think that nobody could dodge the work they're expected to do. Then I set them a written task, putting adjectives after the nouns . . . and they spin this out really slowly, right up to the point where I say 'I'll look at these tonight and give you them back tomorrow.' As soon as there's a deadline, in this case about fifteen more minutes of writing, the atmosphere changes and they get down to writing. Was it something I said?

(Primary-school teacher)

Over a period of time the two teachers and I developed a number of features we believed essential to create strong feedback expectancy. These resulted from our interpretation of pupil behaviour. Children appeared to be more involved, but longer-term study would be needed to confirm these essentials, if indeed it could. The two teachers thought that feedback expectancy was an important feature of pupils' successes. In an interview one of them commented:

TEACHER: I think that a strong expectation that feedback will be needed at various stages of an activity is very powerful. It's a powerful incentive in the learning process and certainly I get quite excited about the concept myself.

RB: Thinking about the usual pattern, the way you went about asking for feedback, is there anywhere you think you created a habit?

TEACHER: A little way into the activity, children expected we would stop and discuss further planning. 'How are you and your group tackling this task? What d'you think you'll learn?' Then teasing out a set of criteria or key elements of learning. They're all expected to participate. They know they would look mighty silly if they hadn't a clue at this stage. A bit further into the task we'd also from time to time have a whole group forum. There was always the expectation that feedback would be required and each member of the group would have to be prepared to present or give feedback on how it was going. And they'd have to answer questions from us. At the end of an activity there was always the expectation that some write-up would be needed and there would be a clear deadline for doing this. Feedback from us was also expected at this stage. In most cases we'd expect feedback from the children in their evaluations. Really, on reflection, I realise the importance of children knowing that their feedback helps teachers in their future planning. It's useful for them as pupils, of course. 'Another time I will present it differently', or whatever.

RB: You said, 'It's an incentive.' Can you say a bit more about that?

TEACHER: As far as motivation is concerned, I think it's pretty clear that children soon realised that they really needed to be very involved with the task so they could give feedback to anybody . . . someone who wanted to talk about their work. Now that must be a very powerful incentive indeed.

Apart from signalling those points at which feedback was regularly demanded, teaching this way presumes there is discussion with pupils. It would be speculation if I suggested that feedback expectancy alone can strongly influence learning. It is well known that a variety of other factors affect pupil progress. The pacing of lessons, quality of planning and learning potential of tasks, classroom management and motivation are further features known to influence effective teaching and learning (Brophy and Good 1986; Bennett et al. 1984; Doyle 1986, 1990). Strong feedback expectancy would be a factor requiring further research in order to determine how significant an overall effect it has on learning.

Effects of intensifying feedback

The teachers reported informally that they had discussed the power of *feedback expectancy* with other colleagues. One of the teachers said, 'At first I thought it was gobbledegook, but I've tested it numerous times since and found it isn't.' He was convinced that this side effect of research into pupil self-assessment was powerful, and he found that the more he built it into his teaching, the stronger pupil expectations seemed to be. Many more pupils than usual were keen to report back because they had already generated material through attending, listening and taking action in readiness to be asked.

Pupils reported in written form on some of the longer self-assessments.

> You can write things you've done. They [assessment forms] help you to speak out what you think.

> Good, because they [assessment forms] made you think what you got out of it.

> You could look back and think about what you had done and the self-assessment diary page enabled you to write other things besides what you did and what you found out.

> It made me think about what I'd done and why I did it. If we evaluated maths, I had to check my sums and now I do it automatically.

> It has helped me keep my confidence up. I look for the information before I start on the work. I write it down in an organised fashion.

> It's helped me to see the improvement I'm making. It's a way of saying to someone, 'This is what I have learned and improved on', and you hand them your self-assessment book. It helps you to learn more and things which you'd like to find out more about.

There were negative effects reported, such as 'assessment fatigue', which was pupil reluctance to assess what they had completed. Responses included:

It makes some things more boring than what they already are because when I come to evaluating a piece of work it makes it boring.

I think it's boring because all we do is kind of doing the same bit of work two times. I would like to be doing a new task or something else than assessment. I don't think most of the class likes doing assessment so what's the point of it?

I don't like self-assessment because it doesn't help me while I could be doing something else. Like now, sitting here doing evaluations when I haven't done my pictures on my story.

I think the self-assessments are not much help because you could be getting on with things like finishing off work.

Teachers in training later said:

You can see by their faces that they're more interested in the task if they know they've some input into what they're doing. And quite often you can build in choices as well for them.

When we watched a video about Henry VIII, they sat still concentrating. I said, 'There are certain things I want you to watch out for and then I'll ask you questions afterwards.' Erm . . . it made them have something to focus on while they were watching rather than just blindly watching it. You've got to know what it is you want them to learn and they [pupils] need to know what they're trying to learn.

Well, I think that telling them they would report back kept them focused on a specific point and they knew they would have to come back to that later, so it kept their attention more. I think it's difficult because some children you'll miss anyway, because they switch off, but you can target specific questions. I'd say, 'Jason, I'm coming back to you later, so remember', and make it more specific. It's worth doing because it engages the children's attention more fully if they know they're going to have to come back to you later. Otherwise they can just switch off.

I'd say targets are useful definitely. Written-down targets are there and the children can see them. Something specific. 'By the end of the lesson I want you to, etc.' Towards the end of the lesson, they're beginning to buzz about it and [say], 'Have you done it yet?' Conversation between them as to whether they've done it or not.

(Interviews)

Did they do this *always, completely* with *everything*? Certainly not. There are limits to increasing expectations that pupils will write down their feedback. For some pupils, 'self-assessment fatigue' may set in. Short and simple verbal feedback was far more popular with the class. A drawback of this was that it did not give pupils or teachers much time to reflect on feedback. Longer-term self-assessments were needed for this. In our project, we found that pupil self-assessment sets in motion a chain of events that can be dynamic, rewarding for teachers and effective as a means of involving pupils in their learning. In particular, strong expectations of feedback can focus what already takes place and intensify its positive effects. Pupils do better because they are involved. If they do better as a result of becoming involved, this can lead to a spiral of success. They gain feedback from successful involvement and are further motivated to be involved as a result.

KEY POINTS

- A self-defeating belief is that *because* pupils want things to be done easily, without effort, there *should* therefore be an easy, magical way to do them.
- If things are hard, that is the way they often are – hard.
- Recognising that some beliefs are self-defeating is, in itself, very positive.
- Most active involvement includes feedback from pupils and teachers or from learning tasks themselves.
- In formative feedback there can be strong and weak expectations.
- Strong expectations of feedback can focus what already takes place and intensify its positive effects on pupils' involvement.
- Feedback expectancy involves conscripts as well as volunteers.
- Pupils cannot self-assess *always*, *completely* and for *everything*.
- Building in *feedback expectancy* can drive forward activity and focus concentration.

Chapter 5

Pupil self-assessment and positive outcomes

Feeding back into learning

Planning for assessment that feeds back into learning (formative assessment) has always been part of a teacher's job, but not always one carried out systematically. Paul Black and Dylan Wiliam (1998) of King's College, London, found in a world-wide survey of schools that formative feedback, especially if systematic, was successful in achieving improved learning (O'Connor 1998: 22). Formative assessment has a valued and acknowledged role, even though it is difficult to implement well. Black and Wiliam provide a checklist of what they think works:

- regular classroom testing and the use of results to adjust teaching and learning, rather than competitive grading;
- enhanced feedback between the teacher and the taught which may be oral or in the form of written comments on work;
- the active involvement of all pupils;
- careful attention to the motivation and self-esteem of pupils, encouraging them to believe that they can learn what is being taught;
- time allowed for self-assessment by pupils, discussion in groups and dialogue between teachers and pupils.

(O'Connor 1998: 22)

Once again, this sounds so familiar that we may believe we already do it. The summary checklist is peppered with words and phrases like 'careful attention', 'regular testing' and 'time allowed for self-assessment', which give little idea of what they mean in practice. Key words we can hang on to are 'enhanced feedback', which suggest that formative assessment is planned for, rather than left to chance. In planned and systematic formative assessment, feedback is not only given, but its frequency and quality are much improved. One of its intentions is to include supportive measures to improve pupils' learning abilities. Systematic formative assessment is intended to be positive, supportive and constructive. If it is truly supportive it helps pupils to learn, rather than giving cautionary report cards on their ability, esteem, sense of self or personal worth. It is healthy enough to rate effort and performance, but self-assessment could easily become a guilt-trip of self-downing criticism. The difficulty is that however carefully a teacher avoids assessment as a rating, pupils may still want to rate themselves.

Here is the devil in the detailed practice. In theory, pupils can decide some of the criteria they need to produce high-quality work and later assess to what extent these are achieved. The reality in our research project (summarised in Chapter 4) was very different. Self-assessment involved pupils, but there were limits to their understanding of it. Children's knowledge of formative assessment is inevitably less sophisticated than that of their teachers. This proved to be true even when pupils were taught ways to self-assess. In our experience, children did their best, but were not immediately aware of what the results meant. They knew where they had difficulties, but not what to do next to put them right. At the start of our project, pupils' assessment data tended to be opinions about what they liked, what they thought they got out of the work they did, and a few wild guesses about how to improve. This can be useful feedback for teachers, but it is questionable what might be done for a pupil who reports 'I didn't like this' or 'I didn't understand, it was too difficult'. Pupils need higher-level understanding of self-assessment if it is to be worth doing.

The purpose of self-assessment goes far beyond assessing to make pupils feel involved in their learning. Formative assessment is concerned with how judgements about pupil responses can be used to shape future teaching and learning. A central intention is to short-circuit 'the randomness and inefficiency of trial-and-error learning' (Sadler 1989: 120). Pupils might, for example, submit and discuss their early drafts of text in English so as to allow their teachers to identify progress or diagnose difficulties. Teachers might look at pupil self-assessments in mathematics and revise their teaching about area or place-value. The aim of formative assessment is to set up a means of gaining useful feedback as quickly as is necessary for the situation.

Summative assessment, by comparison with formative assessment, is relatively passive. Its function is to provide judgements as measures of effectiveness, competence or achievement at a given stage. Summative assessment is concerned with summing up outcomes, often testing, assigning grades, and reporting at the end of a task or period of study. It is not designed to impact directly and actively on teaching and learning as they take place. Summative assessment can be used to certificate pupils and to make comparisons between pupils of a similar age. Its primary purpose is to monitor outcomes, often on a national basis through public examinations or statutory tests. Its importance and dominance within educational settings are due to its place within formal statutory assessment requirements for the purposes of establishing comparative 'standards' against criteria for achievement.

Why formative assessment is hard, but not impossible

Teachers often find it extremely difficult to accommodate information from the outcomes of formative assessment. Sometimes what is found out comes too late or cannot be used to influence learning. Although feedback from formative assessment is thought to help teachers in their planning, the general research picture is one of neglect (Black 1995: 7; Black and Wiliam 1998). There is no extensive track record of pupils implementing formative assessment, and not enough evaluation of how it might be done. The simple rules for success do not exist, except as general advice derived from studies such as that of Black and Wiliam. Not only is there neglect of research, but formative assessment is also easily eclipsed by other demands. When is all this to be fitted into an over-crowded day? The assessment priorities tend to be those that enhance success in summative assessments, often for the purposes of making comparisons between pupils, schools, areas of the country and countries themselves. Where summative outcomes become the main focus, the tendency is to concentrate on those aspects that are easy to test, with the effect of lowering the cognitive level of classroom work (Black 1995: 7). In an over-loaded educational agenda, items that are not statutorily required, or not easy to compare, are likely to be pushed aside in favour of those that are.

A more pressing difficulty for teachers is that formative assessment information has to be acted on or it was not worth gathering in the first place. Summative assessment data can remain as recorded grades or information and need not necessarily lead to action. This can be a further reason why formative assessment is so neglected. It may just be an aspiration that teachers adjust their plans as a result of formative assessments. What if teachers are in no position to take action as a result of formative assessment? The future tasks implied by formative data may be too hard to do, or require too much additional time. If teachers are aware of their possible inability to act on the evidence, this militates against data being collected. Formative assessment may need to fit the present or imminent teaching and learning. Consequently there can be unreasonable deadlines to be met if feedback is going to be used. A teacher puts it like this:

> Formative assessment's a good thing, but it's the first item to fall off the back of the educational cart because we've so many other pressing things to do. So I *say* I do formative assessment all the time. Actually, I'm more likely to worry about what assessment reveals, because I'll probably have to do something about it. If I leave formative assessment as informal as possible then I can respond to children there and then, and not be bogged down in the detail. I don't want to create a mountain of work for myself, simply because I've assessed formally with the idea of improving their learning. It's no good doing this for some vague and distant future lessons, so there's the

added pressure of a deadline to be met. Result? I didn't want to plan for formative assessment so of course it didn't happen.

(Primary-school teacher)

Formative assessment clearly has its inherent downside. It may reveal the impossible tasks ahead for pupil and teacher, a list of 'should do', 'must complete by Wednesday', and 'must do better'. Aside from these anxieties, improvements of pupils' achievement through formative assessment are not inevitable. Faced by all of this, do we just give up and forget about it?

The indispensable conditions for improvement are 'that the student [that is, pupil] comes to hold a concept of quality roughly similar to that held by the teacher' (Sadler 1989: 121).

> Stated explicitly, the learner has to (a) possess a concept of the *standard* (or goal or reference level) being aimed for, (b) compare the *actual* (or current) *level of performance* with the standard, and (c) engage in appropriate *action* which leads to some closure of the gap [between the actual and the standard or reference levels].
>
> (Sadler 1989: 121)

Sadler's view is that for assessment to be formative it must bring about a change for the person who is assessed. Such a view, however, is like saying that a medicine is not a medicine unless it makes the patient better. Assessment can actually be formative by intention and purpose, whether or not it subsequently changes the pupil. It can be fed back by teachers to other individuals and groups, but it is a questionable assumption to suppose it is always bound to lead to change.

If formative assessment is such a good practice, how can it successfully be implemented? We found in our research with 10-year-old pupils that formative assessment was possible given the six essential ingredients listed below.

Six essential ingredients of self-assessment

- Shared understanding of teaching and learning aims.
- Timetabled opportunities for written self-assessment.
- Timetabled feedback on these, or written replies to pupils.
- Strong expectations (feedback expectancy).
- Praise for effort, not for grading.
- A further means of communication such as a message-box or 'help-slip tin'.

Not surprisingly, this list of ingredients is mainly about communication and feedback. The first ingredient is perhaps the most important from a teaching perspective. We took considerable trouble to share our aims. Pupils gathered around to discuss what we were trying to achieve, they said what they thought was useful and heard further explanations. We knew very early on that we would need to plan time for feedback on this and we found a good time was either at the start or after about ten minutes into the session. We had already had an example of what happens when assessment is not well timetabled. In the early days of pupil self-assessment, I had devised a simple checklist (Figure 5.1). The text within each box is an example of what the pupils wrote. The self-assessment forms were initially very popular with the pupils because they could use them whenever they wished. They had control over them, and seemed to like them because they were simple. In the end, they were forgotten, or the task pupils had decided to assess did not happen that day. Few pupils managed to fill in the section that said 'Action'. We quickly discovered that leaving assessment to pupils was not going to work. Like any other human beings, they had other concerns and there was no reminder to do assessments. More importantly there was no deadline and no specified time for feeding back to teachers or using them in a session. Self-assessments like these produced comments like 'try harder', 'do it more neatly', which were almost exactly what pupils had heard as classroom rules and exhortations by their teachers. Pupils' self-assessments sometimes clashed with their teacher's priorities. A pupil, for example, might decide to improve the general layout of writing in English, when the teacher was more concerned with rough draft of content.

Name:	Class: Date:
Task: Group work Making a torch	**Goal:** To improve my questions and discuss more with the rest of my group.
Action: Listen more before I speak Try harder next time	**Self-assessment** 1 ☐ Brilliant 2 ☐ Special 3 ☑ Good 4 ☐ Average 5 ☐ Poor 6 ☐ The worst

Figure 5.1 The simple data sheet

The main advantage of this simple self-assessment sheet was that pupils could understand it. The disadvantages were that they forgot to use it if it was not part of the timetabled day. Items to be assessed were often naive.

Trying out goals concerned with effort, understanding and skill

One of the better ideas to emerge from this assessment sheet concerned pupil praise. We found we could praise goals that were to do with skills like listening and working hard in a group. This, it may be remembered, is what Mueller and Dweck (1998) cited as being the value of praising effort, rather than praising intelligence or ability (Chapter 4). Pupils in Mueller and Dweck's study, who were praised for effort rather than ability, chose more challenging work and were more tenacious in the face of failure.

An example of processes requiring effort came in a practical task that pupils did. They were asked to draw a plan for a house, and we listed their four 'Key elements of learning' as:

1   Taking measurements of rooms.
2   Recording data for use later.
3   Developing observation skills.
4   Doing a survey of the region around the house.

When they self-assessed these learning elements, and discussed their assessments in a period of time designated for this, we again concentrated on praising effort. We gave importance to the processes of working. We asked, 'How well did you record data?' but expected the results to reflect hard work and effort, not a rating. When later asked what the strong elements in self-assessment might be, the two teachers responded:

JC: Looking very closely at what they are getting out of something. Not in a surface sort of way like 'I am doing my sums correctly' but 'Am I able to work in this way? Am I able to work independently? Do I need help? Do I need to bounce ideas off someone else?' Just looking closely at the process of working perhaps.

JE: I agree with that and I think there's been increased motivation on our part and their part with identifying what is the learning going on. I mean, we have identified in the past what elements of those activities we were interested in, but because we haven't communicated those to the children in the past, we have just assumed that they will gain those by *doing*.

Self-assessment, where we felt it to be most successful, dealt with 'learning to learn'. Pupils' executive organising and learning skills were being developed, though for a time they wanted to include a self-grade. See Figures 5.2–5.4.

Date: Individual/group	Self-evaluation of Siege Project Task: Accommodation plan	Name:		Y6
Key elements of learning	**Nat Curric Ats**	**Write here about how well you performed**	**Self-assessment**	**Help needed?**
1 Understanding the problem	**Maths AT 9**	There were a lot of problems but our group did well, e.g. had trouble with our scale.	6/10	No
2 Effective use of space	**Maths AT 9**	Our ideas for the space we had worked very well, e.g. spaced the beds evenly.	8/10	No
3 Recording ideas clearly	**Maths AT 9**	We recorded our idea very clearly on a big bit of paper.	7/10	No
4 Describing plans to the Year Group	**Maths AT 9 English AT 1**	We described our plan in great detail and it was good.	9/10	No
Further study:	I intend to find out more about: I intend to develop these skills further			Fill in 'help' slip where you need further help.

Figure 5.2 Self-assessment schedule: Accommodation plan

Date: Individual/group	Self-evaluation of Siege Project Task: Safety and first-aid duty		Name:		Y6
Key elements of learning	**Nat Curric Ats**	**Write here what you know and understand**	**Self-assessment**		**Help needed?**
1 Approaching an accident patient	**Science AT 3**	First if the patient has tables and chairs on them you have to get them out of the way. Then if they are not breathing you blow into their mouth two times then you press 5 times then blow into their mouth again.	10/10		No
2 Finding out the history of the accident	**Science AT 3 English AT 1**	What you have to do is first ask what happened, but if they can't speak look around the room.	8/10		No
3 First-aid treatment of patient	**Science AT 3**	The treatment that I did on the patient was the right thing to do.	10/10		No
4 Calling for medical assistance	**Science AT 3 English AT 1**	If someone was hurt I could call 999 and keep calm.	10/10		No
Further study:	**I intend to find out more about:** **I intend to develop these skills further**		**Fill in 'help' slip where you need further help.**		

Figure 5.3 Self-assessment schedule: Safety and first-aid duty

| Date: | Self-evaluation of Siege Project | Name: | | Y6 |
| Individual/group | Task: Newspaper craft | | | |
Key elements of learning	Nat Curric Ats	Write here how well you performed	Self-assessment	Help needed?
1 Testing out paper folding ideas	Des & Tech AT 2	We tried to make a bridge, snooker table, swords and a bird table but they didn't work.	2/10	Yes
2 Making strong structures from paper	Science AT 6 & 10	I can't make strong structures just from paper and I need help.	3/10	Yes
3 Describing how to make an object to someone else	English AT 1	I described the things I made very well in conference.	6/10	No
4 Joining paper without the use of glue, Sellotape, etc.	Des & Tech AT 3	You can make paper strong from getting strips of paper and tying round it.	7/10	No
Further study:	I intend to find out more about:		Fill in 'help' slip where you need further help.	
	I intend to develop these skills further			

Figure 5.4 Self-assessment schedule: Newspaper craft

We did not use schedules as elaborate as these very often. The search for faster means of feedback prompted two further ways of assessing. One was through a five-minute assessment on scrap paper using three sections (Figure 5.5). These could alternatively be done by drawing three circles, using three separate pieces of paper. Here we have used three columns in which to categorise. Trainee-teachers who have used these since have described them as being fast, simple and effective feedback on their teaching.

What I understand	Think I know	Don't understand/ know
Verbs	Adverbs	Pronouns
Nouns	Conjunctions	Prepositions
Adjectives		

Figure 5.5 Grammar check

Using help-slips for communicating

One of the problems for pupils learning anything is being left behind during explanations. Another is doing a task, but wanting further help. A solution the two teachers devised was to make photocopied 'help-slips' which were to be used by pupils to tell their teachers what was confusing or needed further attention. On a table at the side of the classroom we put a tin with a slot cut into the lid. All children were given photocopied sheets of help-slips on which they filled in their name and the help they needed. They were told that the tin operated like a secret ballot in that other pupils would not be able to read the help-slips. They were also told that written comments such as 'I'm hopeless at maths' were not going to be very useful. Help-slips needed to be specific.

The effect of help-slips can be compared to using email. Brief messages are stored until the tin is opened and the message read. Instant and brief replies are usual. The examples (Figures 5.6–5.9) show some requests for help.

Name: Lisa   **Group:** H

Task: Launcher

I need help with: Making my launcher shoot direct

Figure 5.6 Help-slip: Launcher

Name: Kevin   **Group:** B

Task: Poster design

I need help with: Keeping a steady
hand with a brush. I need help
with painting colours so they
don't run

Figure 5.7 Help-slip:
Poster design

Name: Clare   **Group:** H

Task: Making a torch

I need help with: How electric
current flows round a circuit

Figure 5.8 Help-slip:
Making a torch

Name: Richard **Group:** G

Task: Music

I need help with: I don't understand
rhythm and pitch

Figure 5.9 Help-slip: Music

Several examples of help needed are listed below. One was a cry for help. 'The group won't let me do any circuit work' (spelled 'the grop wont let me do ene sekit werk').

I need help with the nails because I hit my finger, not the nail.

I need help with drawing circuit diagrams with symbols.

I need help with writing the rhythm down.

Writing down musical parts. You don't do it like at orchestra.

I don't know what rhythm and tempo mean.

How does the bulb light up when we put the wire on?

I need help with sawing wood.

At first, we thought we would be inundated with requests for help. There was no pressure on pupils to fill in help-slips, but every pupil had at least a dozen of these in their desk ready to use if they wanted to. In practice, requests for help tended to be concerned with the last five or six activities the children had done. The teachers created two gaps on the timetable for help sessions and an hour was allocated to this each Tuesday and Friday. Help-slips that concerned the same topic suggested a need for further teaching. In informal discussion, children revealed that whereas they would not want to admit to difficulties if in earshot of their friends, they were much more inclined to use help-slips. Pupils in our study said that they liked the secrecy and the opportunity a help-slip provided.

There were practical reasons why responses to help-slips had to be limited. We created the time for assessment whenever we could. Our concern to encourage more extensive, specific assessments meant that the use of help-slips was initially played down. We had no desire to see a classroom where the teaching was being driven by help-slips, or one where we felt under unreasonable pressure to respond. Not every activity could therefore be monitored with assessment schedules because of the time this took, but help-slips could be used for responding to anything of concern to the pupils.

Some effects of help-slips

When help-slips were grouped together, we were surprised about two features in particular. First, when we asked for the fifteen pupils who needed help with electric circuits, only nine responded. On being questioned, they said that they had been talking to their friends since putting in the help-slip and now they felt they understood. This was by no means uncommon and is an intriguing aspect of using help-slips. I had noticed early on the alarming speed with which children seemed to abandon all thoughts of their lesson once it was over. Though it is never possible to be certain about this, to our knowledge they did not revisit their difficulties unless prompted to do so. The shutters of the mind appeared to come down and the children had little idea when the subject-matter might surface again. As soon as help-slips were introduced, instead of misunderstandings remaining in the distant past, there was the chance to revisit them later in the week. Pupils might not take that chance, and the revisiting might be overlooked, but at least the opportunity was there.

We found that a distinction can be made between feedback of a low-level, self-correcting kind, and feedback that triggers discussion. Low-level feedback could be about classroom rules and routines such as 'Check your addition before you finish' and 'Look at the spelling to see if you copied it correctly'. High-level feedback could trigger discussion of scientific concepts such as 'understanding evaporation' or 'the reasons for temperature change in materials'. Towards the end of the research project it was possible to interview almost every child concerning self-assessment. Here are some pupils' responses to the question 'What have you found useful and why?':

Help-slips. Because if you were stuck it sorts it out.

Help-slips. Because before these, you had to see a member of staff, but this is a good way to get messages to them.

Now they [the teachers] explain it more, so we don't need them.

Help-slips. Really useful because you can get help.

If you get stuck you feel shy and you can put it [a slip] in the tin.

Help-slips were good because [later on] we went in another room and they told you what was going on.

Help-slips are OK. Sometimes you need help, but you don't know what it is.

You could get more help. You could learn more because you had extra help.

A surprise was that pupils saw help-slips as useful whether they actually were or not, in some cases believing they were a source of extra help. Help-slips could remind a teacher that the pupils' needs for further help still existed. A further possibility was that by having to wait for help, the pupil might continue to chew over the problem from time to time. It is not possible to know about this conclusively without access to a pupil's stream of consciousness, but the possibility remains. By contrast, several pupils later reported that self-assessments were becoming a chore, just another piece of work to do. Analysing their responses over a number of assessments, however, we found a wide range of responses. Some pupils had difficulty writing more than the minimum response, such as 'Can't do that very well', 'Can do that well'.

Extending and sustaining self-assessments

One of the main problems we picked up was that some less able pupils were not giving reasons for what they said. Their responses were very brief and limited compared with other pupils. We made a concerted effort to encourage pupils to give reasons, and we described this as using the word 'because'. We wanted to extend pupils' ability to reason, an aim already well-documented as worthwhile by educators such as Lipman (1991), De Bono (1991), Paul (1987) and others concerned with pupils' thinking. The teachers later turned the 'because' device into a more extensive form, displayed on a flipchart as key words. These were intended to provoke specific and extensive responses.

because	I looked for
but	We also
so	I also
then	

Table 5.1 Assessment methods

Assessment method	Characteristics	Mode of reflection
Self-assessment schedules Longer-term and criterion-referenced against 'Key elements of learning'	Pupils are expected to respond in written form and give reasons. These are specific and detailed assessment instruments. The teacher is expected to respond. Feedback between pupils and teachers is a feature of response intended to generate formative action. (Teacher response is longer-term, possibly more than 5 days.)	Time needed by the pupil to complete the written response. Time needed by the teacher to respond to the pupil (possibly in written form).
Conferencing	Pupils in a small group engage in dialogue with teacher about their work and metacognitive strategies. Action proposed by pupil and/or teacher. (Teacher response is immediate.)	Interactive dialogue needed, but reflection is brief and is engaged in at the time.
Weekly review of pupils' learning	Whole class discussion, unless there are too many pupils. Alternatively, written responses may be invited from pupils. Can be a session where teachers review their claims about the teaching covered. Self-assessment may be a strong or weak feature. Formative feedback possible.	Reflection at the time, but can promote longer-term reflection if pupil or teacher finds content invites this.

Help-slips *Three columns* (also quizzes, slip-tests and rapid peer testing)	Feedback to signal help needed. Some identification of problems possible. Act as bookmarks for unresolved or unfinished aspects of tasks and/or understanding. Strongly orientated towards the teacher as responder. (1–5-day response is usual.)	Believed to promote some reflection from the pupil, after being filled in, and before the teacher gives a response.
Pupil–teacher task dialogue, self-assessing and giving verbal feedback	Ongoing feedback before, during tasks. Informal and reactive. Can involve considerable correction by others and some consequent self-correction. [During sessions]	Reflection is briefly engaged in at the time. Reflection may be longer-term as a result of dialogue.
Informal self-monitoring	Self-correcting immediately, e.g. correcting an explanation.	Little chance to reflect.

Italics have been added to the following example of a pupil's written feedback. This is to show where the pupil extends comments. Some pupils wrote about problems they had working in groups.

> Board Games. I think Juliette's was the best *because* it was wonderful and you could understand it easily and for an 8-year-old would be able to answer the questions and understand how to play. If we made another game I wouldn't make it with the boys *because* they leave us out. I got on well with the people I went around with. I would like to make another one.

There are three main demands made on a teacher's time in order to implement formative assessment. First, time is needed to design a schedule that covers the activity in terms of its 'Key elements of learning'. Second, there needs to be time to read and reflect on the pupils' self-assessments. Third, time must be set aside to engage in dialogue with individuals to improve understanding and feed back suggestions for further learning. This is not all extra work. Most involves a shift of priorities. Designing a schedule can probably be absorbed into a teacher's lesson planning, and may have the advantage of clarifying aims. The remaining time commitments would need to be weighed against other priorities.

The following are 'sustainable findings' from our research. After a year, the two teachers in the research project still found it true that:

- Long tasks, such as projects and topics stretching over days, are more appropriate for self-assessment than short ones because breaking off from longer tasks to assess is less intrusive.
- Specifying in advance what the majority of pupils could achieve is useful for rapid assessment later on.
- Rapid feedback instruments such as the 'three columns' can be sustained.
- Planning for formative assessment can be *systematic* in a teaching programme.

Table 5.1 on pages 78 and 79 provides a summary of formative assessment methods.

In implementing pupil self-assessment an advantage for teachers is that it provides data which they themselves do not have to collect. The data can also trigger reflection about learning for both teachers and pupils. A disadvantage is that, in order for the feedback loop to be completed between teacher and pupil, some of the data must actually be seen by teachers, reflected on and fed back. Otherwise pupils' misunderstandings could go unnoticed. This clearly takes time. However, we found that pupils may experience assessment fatigue if they do not have reciprocal feedback or if there is an overload of assessment. Some pupils reported in our study that the very act of self-assessment clarified what they were trying to do and this resulted in self-correction. The main message for me was that it was not enough to use pupil self-assessment now and again. It was not enough to self-assess infrequently. Self-assessment was at its most powerful when it was part of the day, planned for and expected.

KEY POINTS

- Formative assessment is hard, but not impossible to do.
- It must be systematically planned for, or it will tend to be superficial.
- If it is not planned, there are no realistic deadlines for feedback.
- The process of pupil self-assessment, followed by feedback, can clarify a teacher's targets for pupil achievement.
- Formative assessment encourages active involvement by pupils.
- It provides opportunities for the teacher to give constructive encouragement and minimise misunderstandings.
- It can sharply focus teaching aims and objectives in preparation for sharing these with pupils.
- Help-slips are a useful means of communication.
- Pupil self-assessment is limited by pupils' ability to analyse what they are doing. Self-assessments need to be specific.
- Formative assessment promotes pupil reflection on teaching and learning.

Chapter 6

Using descriptive praise

It seems crazy to suggest that praise has ever been anything but an essential ingredient of teaching. Who could disagree? Almost every teacher I have met has something to say about praise. I have heard teachers say, 'These children need lots of praise and encouragement' and I believe them. The trouble is that children can react in very different ways to praise. Praise is a reward, and if a teacher praises, the pupil is high in their esteem. Some children will become so dependent on receiving praise that they regard its absence as failure. Praise can centre the attention of children on themselves, rather than on what action is to be taken next (Dreikurs *et al.* 1982). A child might wonder, 'How do I measure up?' instead of 'What does the situation need?' If children are convinced that what they did was nowhere near their idea of 'excellent', a teacher's praise could become a mockery. There are adults for whom receiving praise when they were a child was more like taking poison.

> My parents always praised me for everything I did. You would think the result of that would be to make me confident and positive. Nothing of the sort! They meant well, but they praised so much that it just made me angry. There were times when I knew what I had done did not deserve praise and I could see praise on its way towards me, signifying nothing. Things I had done were nearly always 'brilliant, wonderful and fabulous'. Often, I would stand there waiting for the expected praise as if I was about to take some foul-tasting and thoroughly nasty medicine.
>
> (Family therapist)

> My parents rarely praised me. There was always a 'but you could do this better' or 'make sure next time that you remember this or that'. If not accompanied by a 'but', then there was a negative nit-picky comparison with other children down the street, or my weaknesses were quickly pointed out rather than my achievements. So things I did were never ever good enough. I resented what little praise there was because it was given begrudgingly. I suppose it's made me determined not to give up easily, but with that has

come a perfectionism I could well live without. It's made me a bit critical of myself and others. I've had to recognise that and learn to be better at giving praise to children.

(Primary-school teacher)

Over-praising and the absence of praise are extremes. The former can be insincere and the latter over-balance to signal very negative feedback. These two adult memories curiously have one feature in common, which is that they both diminish the child because their praise message was unrealistic, generalised and in the form of a judgement or a rating. Telling a pupil 'You are a brilliant writer' boosts their confidence only if they believe it. All that may happen is that they are reminded of all the times they were not brilliant (Faber and Mazlish 1995). It is very hard to accept extravagant praise that judges a child rather than describes achievement. Even in the absence of praise, there can be implied judgement as the eternal phrase 'could do better' resonates in the mind.

Descriptive praise is quite different from this. I prefer to think of it as 'non-negative thinking', which describes rather than judges. Some research already shows that our explanatory style has a significant effect on how we view our successes and failures (Seligman 1990). If a teacher's explanatory style, the way they describe events, is defeatist and they see weaknesses before strengths, their classroom perception will reflect this. It may even become emotionally draining for the teacher who uses it. As I pointed out in Chapter 2, an explanatory style full of self-talk like 'I *never* get it right', 'It's *always* going wrong' is global, pervasive and personal. Although it is also irrational, and therefore far removed from reality, it is an understandable expression of frustration. Unfortunately, it may lead an individual to think, 'Nothing I do ever matters, so why bother to make the effort?' As Bernard (1990) points out, a teacher's overly pessimistic explanatory style is actually a powerful feature of teacher stress. I would add that it could be a barrier to praising children.

An antidote to a pessimistic explanatory style is to relearn how to describe events and achievements. An obvious objection to this is that a positive description encourages an unrealistic, rose-tinted view of the world. I strongly disagree. A natural tendency to be negative means that many perceptions are already far removed from reality. The remainder of this chapter includes suggestions about handling pupils' errors, dealing with necessary negative feedback and keeping a child's self-esteem intact.

There are five reasons why learning descriptive praise is worthwhile:

1   Descriptive praise allows pupils to credit themselves.
2   It does not ignore errors.
3   It can help teachers and pupils see the positive features in what they do.
4   The school day can be a much more positive experience.
5   It is also honest.

Descriptive praise has been written about for a number of years, particularly by those concerned with therapy and behaviour management (Faber and Mazlish 1980, 1995; Rogers 1992; Rollinson 1997; Humphreys 1993). Like many other classroom processes, feedback as descriptive praise is not new. Its development and power lie in learning to fine-tune specific descriptions of achievement. It minimises global judgements like 'great' and 'brilliant' in favour of detail related specifically to what is going on. Describing, rather than judging, is very powerful indeed because it focuses on actual evidence of achievement and effort put in. This leaves the pupil a chance to credit themselves by saying, 'Yes I *did* do that carefully and I completed that well.' A flavour of descriptive praise can be seen in the following teacher comments:

I like the way you co-operated when working together, which meant you achieved a lot more and your results were better than if you hadn't.

You had to write about a trip to the supermarket and this could have been boring. But you took care over the details and included some conversation about the delicatessen, which made it much more imaginative.

You concentrated so hard on that, you didn't stop for a second before you finished.

I noticed that the way you use your brush shows me you thought about how you wanted it to look on paper. That's helped you get the effect you wanted to achieve.

I like the way your picture is different from everyone else's, which shows you really thought about it for yourself.

Your picture is interesting because you thought about the materials you were going to use, which famous artists take great care over.

You made good use of the space on the paper by the careful way you laid out your work.

The extra time you put into this is really paying off.

You have two hands on your paper, which is helping you to hold the paper still as you write.

You've chosen special words to describe things and that's making your writing much more interesting to read.

I notice you used a sharp pencil to get those co-ordinates accurate. You understood how to start and finish your graph so that someone else could make sense of it.

I used the words 'transparent', 'translucent' and 'opaque' and you remembered the difference by the end of the week. Well done.

Now that you can use the graph program on the computer, I can see you will be able to show someone else. You got quicker using the mouse and you checked your typing of the data to see if it was accurate.

You understood the diagram of a circuit and joined the wires, battery and bulb so we could add a switch.

The information on your chart is easy to recognise because it has clear labels.

You've thought about safety and used plastic goggles and gloves. I didn't need to remind you.

If we want to encourage persistence and tenacity, it is important to understand the difference between praise that rates children and that which encourages them. In a study I have already mentioned in Chapter 4, some children were told, 'Wow, that's a really good score, you must be really smart at this.' Others were told, 'Wow, that's a really good score, you must have worked really hard.' Persistence was evident in the group praised for working hard. Persistence fell away from those children praised for being intelligent as soon as they experienced failure. They saw intelligence as fixed, and tended to look for tasks in which they could succeed, rather than challenging tasks from which they could learn (Mueller and Dweck 1998). Children, as Faber and Mazlish (1995) put it, tend to become very uncomfortable with praise that evaluates them as people. 'They push it away. Sometimes they will deliberately misbehave to prove you wrong.' Praise that rates can make children doubt themselves. 'If I was brilliant this time, what will I be like next time?'

We can look again at the list of examples already provided in this chapter. It is not difficult to find plenty of implied judgements, but isolated global judgements, such as 'brilliant', are absent. There is really no such thing as value-free praise because teachers inevitably transmit their personal values. Even when saying something descriptive like 'I notice there's quite a lot of litter on the floor', a judgement about the rightness or otherwise of leaving litter is implied. The actual comment is what counts, and, in this instance, it invites action that is based on a classroom rule about tidiness at the end of a lesson. Where encouragement of effort is concerned, we have a comment like 'The extra time you put into this is really paying off.'

Many of the teachers I regard as being positive frequently use the global words 'brilliant', 'excellent', 'outstanding' and 'fabulous'. They will continue to do so, and most likely so will I. It would be difficult to become a member of the 'Ban the Use of "Brilliant" Club' without praise becoming stilted and losing its spontaneity. Positive teachers (a global evaluation, if ever there was one) rarely say 'brilliant' and leave it at that. *Saying something is 'brilliant' simply does not carry enough information by itself.* 'Brilliant' is irrational, uncomfortable and sometimes embarrassing for pupils because nobody is brilliant always and for everything. If we say 'that was brilliantly done', meaning this time, it needs backing up with a word or two describing the features of a global 'brilliant'. Otherwise it can be misread. Descriptive praise is not 'That's outstanding!' but 'That really looks as if you gave it your best this time. You have a detailed description of an Egyptian temple, using all those special words we talked about and it's paid off. I can tell you're pleased!' Descriptive praise is not 'You're so brilliantly organised', but 'I see you got prepared with pencils, book and your ruler. You sorted the workspace and finished yesterday's work. That must have taken effort.'

If praise is to be effective, then two features of learning how to praise descriptively are important. Both are beliefs, not self-evident truths, but they contrast with soulless, insincere praise.

> Deliberately practising the language of descriptive praise can lead to more spontaneous use of it. Practice is therefore necessary.

> After practising, only what remains ingrained as spontaneous and sincerely felt praise is likely to help children learn. Insincerity undermines teacher–pupil relationships.

One example of practising descriptive praise I like comes from a headteacher who deliberately creates time to observe and praise:

> Not everyone will agree with this, and in any case it doesn't always happen. I think some teachers feel guilty if they are not helping children all the time, but there's an alternative. Once children have begun their tasks, it's helpful just to stand and observe them carefully so you really do have some idea of who's concentrating. I do this for two or three minutes which seems a very long time for a first-school teacher not to be in contact with a child. You might think with little ones this is impossible because they're demanding, but if a child interrupts my observation I'll say, 'Not now, I'm watching carefully.' Actually, I'm looking for things I might praise. It's very important not to say anything at this point or an atmosphere of concentration won't develop. In any case, I want them to realise there's a time to be observed working as well as a time to be helped. I try to find an opportunity to reinforce my intentions through descriptive praise. So I'll say something like 'I notice Sarah has thought carefully about letter shapes' or 'I can see that some of you are trying hard to find special words'. Each time it's a specific learning objective. Whatever it is, it's a golden opportunity to keep the learning objectives in the foreground, observe pupils and practise praising them.

> (First-school headteacher)

What remains as ingrained, spontaneous praise may not amount to much at first. Learning to praise descriptively is like learning a foreign language. When learning to speak French, the nuances of constructing verb tenses can be learned quite deliberately in a class with a teacher. They can even be practised. Correct verb tenses, I have found, can easily disappear when trying to buy a baguette a French bakery. All the construction in the world will not help in moments of panic when the memory deserts. What matters in the end is what remains as a genuine, spontaneous response to being immersed in the language. What remains as a spontaneous language of praise is similarly what counts.

> In the early stages of trying to use descriptive praise I was looking at some policy documents staff had worked on for improving school behaviour. The deputy head had been stressed by the amount of work she was trying to cope with, and she said so as we looked at what she had written. I read what she had put and I still found myself saying to her, 'Yes that's *fine*. Just what we need. Thanks for doing that.' *Fine* is so trivial a judgement to worry over, and anyway it's natural sometimes to say things like that. In learning not to judge, I don't want to end up like the centipede who walked perfectly well until asked which leg went after which . . . so I'm not going to load myself with guilt if I use words like 'good', 'fine', 'excellent' and so on. Once I was aware of saying 'fine' though, I resisted mightily the temptation to judge. I looked more carefully and said, 'You've pulled forward all the main things we were trying to do. I can see how making bullet points helps clarify these into classroom rules and stages of misbehaviour. You've put these in order of importance and it's easy to read. Thanks for taking so much trouble.' Then I thought to myself, 'This descriptive praise stuff isn't working. She doesn't seem praised by me at all!' I was just about to say 'That's brilliant' when I heard a long release of breath. She paused and said, 'That's something I've done well and now I can move on to the next thing.' I could hardly believe it. You have to understand there was no sarcasm from her, nothing but self-praise and release of tension. *She* had said it was done well and she didn't need me to say that because she genuinely believed it for herself. It was a decisive moment for me and she even thanked me as she walked away. And you know the hardest bit? Holding back and stubbornly refusing to say 'brilliant'.
>
> (Headteacher)

That story ties in very closely with an anecdote cited by Faber and Mazlish (1995). Three staff were trying to practise describing children's accomplishments rather than take the easy route of saying 'good' and 'great'. They reported that the hardest part was changing what they were so accustomed to doing. It was one thing to sit at home and decide that this was going to be the week to try out positive description, quite another to go in the next day and do it. In taking the first steps to change classroom explanatory style, I have found that it is worth trying to minimise the use of a global statement such as 'brilliant'. If a 'brilliant' is used, it is only a reminder for me to say more if I possibly can. This does not always happen because of forgetfulness, but the intention is there. In implementing any new ideas, there is normally a dip in effectiveness between the first flush of enthusiasm and the idea becoming internalised. Descriptive praise is no exception to this phenomenon, and forgetting how to praise descriptively is nothing unusual.

Examples and 'I' statements

The role of teacher includes being a corrector of mistakes, which makes it easy to take positive aspects of a child's work and behaviour for granted. It may be even easier to take our own efforts for granted if we rush towards self-criticism. Mistakes can easily demand more attention.

> Children do all kinds of little things without getting noticed for it. The more colourful disruptive and negative things get my attention because they cause problems. Why praise what children already do well? My thinking on this is that it is worth praising to keep them motivated. You have to keep them on your side and descriptive praise helps to do that. Every Friday I go through all the things I think we've achieved during the week and get the pupils to add things too. It's surprising how it mounts up if you include moments of consideration towards each other, moments of real break-through in understanding, pointing out the latest wall display of finished work. You could ignore all that or you could say that you noticed that some child had made the effort despite finding the work difficult. Actually I like to tell them what really excited me and pleased me because it's more of an emotional thing to talk about. When I first started to do this, I couldn't think of many of the small details about their work, but I've got better at it now. Things like 'For three days now, Peter, you remembered to put the books back and clear away your work without a reminder', 'I'm pleased everybody is much quicker at stopping to listen because it's helped me get through the work we needed to do.' If I can, I'll remind them of a specific time during the week 'Do you remember when we . . . ' so it's not just general praise.
>
> (Primary-school teacher)

Handled in an overblown, mechanistic way, praise can easily patronise, depending on the emotion carried by voice-tone. An example of this can be the opportunity for sarcasm imagined in 'You were SO helpful washing the dishes today.' That does not mean examples of praise are not worth including here, but they need adapting to age-range and situation. Most descriptive praise, I have discovered, has five characteristics. Descriptive praise:

1   Avoids one-word global judgements, such as 'brilliant'.
2   Describes appreciatively what can be seen or experienced.
3   Frequently includes or implies the word 'because'.

4   Avoids the word 'but', which cancels what went before.
5   Avoids unnecessary negative focus on weaknesses.

The last two characteristics need explaining. Descriptive praise does not ignore pupils' errors, nor does it rush to point them out. A problem with using the word 'but' within feedback is that it cancels the positive first half of a sentence. Its use does not *always* cancel what went before and cannot *always* be avoided, but it usually has that effect. Some of the intended messages are hidden in a 'but' statement and are extremely negative. Imagine a child's self-talk about what the teacher really might mean: BUT (it isn't ever good enough), BUT (there are too many mistakes), BUT (you are not as good as I want you to be, so you must do better). A negative 'but' is implied by praise like 'I'm really pleased with your writing. Now you must keep it all the same size', or 'Yes, you did very well writing so much. Now when it's really tidy it will be even better.' There is a strong chance that a child will hear mainly the negative criticism and think, 'It isn't tidy enough.' Although this may be the case, a takeaway message of 'it isn't good enough' is not much of a reward for trying. Acknowledging what has been done does not loom so large in the mind. The acknowledgement of achievement and effort is effective only if it is uncontaminated and a 'but' is the contaminator. Praise is effective if it is given unconditionally. As Faber and Mazlish (1980) have commented, 'It's hard to concentrate on what needs to be done when people are telling you what's wrong with you.'

> My father's aged 86 and complains mightily about his aches, pains and difficulty in being able to see properly. That's understandable, but very draining for the rest of us who have to listen time after time. Some days there's no respite from the grumbles and groans because any sympathy offered is not going to be enough. It's much easier to get into an argument about how he's not coping. The other day, I resisted this and instead described his life until he credited himself. I think you have to be careful not to patronise when you do this or it could all go wrong. There's no point in telling him there are people much worse off than he is, because that wouldn't work. I remember from my childhood being told there were people starving in Africa, so I should be grateful to be able to eat up my food. This time I just decided to go on and on describing in a gentle tone of voice, pausing occasionally to see if he would say anything. My script was something like 'You've bought a large-screen television, which is a good idea because you can see more. And since your second eye operation you're not as blurred in vision as you were. You even managed to learn to use Teletext, which not everyone can do, and you operate the remote control. You have a good appetite and you still remember things. The old legs let you get about slowly and you've even been out a few times recently which has helped to break up the week. The heating keeps you warm and a neighbour looks after the garden. There's a weekly shopping trip where you get a lift from your friend

and that helps him get out too.' I didn't need to say much more because he broke into a smile and said 'I suppose I'm not badly off at all!' What's worth trying is just to carry on regardless until there's a better response.

(Teacher)

Describing pupils' errors

It is unreasonable to banish words like 'but' from the English language, and the same goes for words like 'excellent', 'brilliant' and other expressions of appreciation. These are indispensable as in 'Yes. I did forget the meeting, but I usually keep my promises' (Bernard 1990: 279). A crucial feature of handling errors is the balance we achieve between positive and negative description. It goes almost without saying that there needs to be more positive than negative description, but there is one strong reason why this is so. Concentrating on the positive description first can build up enough credit for a pupil to be able to cope with a negative follow-on. Pupils need to have sufficient time to hear and adjust to a positive description (not a judgement) before they are ready for suggestions about improvement. Given a few moments to adjust, they may even come up with improvements themselves.

Here are three examples which praise first, then describe errors. Nothing of what follows can account for voice-tone, hints of good humour or a teacher's pleasure in describing success. An upbeat, appreciative tone of voice is intended here.

> You completed seven maths problems and set them out carefully. Each one was more difficult than the last one and yet you concentrated for a full hour. That means real progress. You had difficulty with numbers five and six. You got these wrong, so we'll need to try to find out why and put that right.

> Your description of the night sky has some special phrases such as 'blurred watery light'. I like that. You set quite an atmosphere when you write about the sounds being louder at night and the wind being cold on your face. The rest of this needs a bit more concentration because there's a sentence here I can't understand. There's a writing problem you need to look at half-way down the page where there looks to be a word missing? You've such an atmosphere in this, see if you can check that last part you wrote and extend it.

> You did *so well* with that! I really like the fact that you found the library books about electricity yourself, thought about these questions you wanted to ask and made a list. You decided in what order to talk about answers to your group and made sure we knew what was important to remember. That's what I call good thinking. I felt really pleased when you completed the circuit and showed everybody what happens when you connect the switch.

Circuits like this one need to be completed with a switch. And you thanked Sarah for helping you too.

The last example began with an appreciative 'You did *so well* with that!' statement, which could be globally judgemental, except for what follows. It is qualified by description so that the pupil is in no doubt that appreciation is meant. Descriptive praise is giving information, such as 'Circuits like this one need to be completed with a switch' or 'Paint brushes need a good wash before we put them away or they'll be difficult to use next time.' Notice in the example about describing the night sky the teacher said 'There's a writing problem' rather than 'You got it wrong'. Two guidelines may help here.

1   Give positive description for long enough to reassure.
2   Describe errors in terms of future action, not just as mistakes made.

It may be possible to reach a stage where the benefits of giving descriptive praise become much more obvious.

> I now notice when I'm *not* using descriptive praise, both in marking and verbally. I've found it so important. Practising descriptive praise forces me to pay close attention to detail about a child's work; it has to be sincere and meaningful, so it has to be accurate. And because the whole point is to be positive, it makes me focus on the good bits – with the equally positive spin-off that I am also clearer about the deficiencies. And I've found over the last term that the things I have been able to write about, such as 'Well done. You've remembered to . . . I can see you have really managed . . . You've worked really hard on . . . ', are the things which then stick for the children, and don't have to be said over and over again.
>
> (Middle-school teacher)

A teacher's 'I' statements are usually safe from the pitfalls of directly judging. Faber and Mazlish (1980) pick up this idea when they point out the difference between saying judgementally 'You did that well' and saying 'I liked the clear voice I heard and your attention to detail'. As an example of a negative realistic response to disruptive behaviour there is a difference between 'You're acting like a wild animal!' and 'I don't like what's going on here'. A teacher can express appreciation or personal feelings by using an 'I' statement. There is a chance to reveal feelings in an honest way. The 'I need' or 'I feel' statements are powerful because they are true. They are true about what I need or feel.

> I really like the way you . . .
>
> I really appreciate that because . . .
>
> I noticed that . . .

I enjoyed . . .

I'm glad you managed to . . .

I'm pleased to say that . . .

I'm delighted it was . . .

I really believe in you . . .

I know you put a lot of effort into that . . .

I value what you just said because it shows . . .

I can see you're upset by . . .

Necessary negative 'I' statements that might be used when there is disruption or off-task, intrusive behaviour:

I don't want you to . . .

I'm not pleased about . . .

I don't like it when . . .

I need you to stop that . . .

I wouldn't like it if . . .

I'm really disappointed with . . .

I don't speak that way to you when . . .

I don't expect . . .

I find it very hard to teach when . . .

I can see a fair number of pieces of paper on the floor. It needs to be clear.

There's a lot of noise here. I need you to . . .

Feelings can be addressed by starting with 'I' statements too:

I noticed you were really frightened then, but you carried on just the same. Well done.

I find that so rewarding, it makes me feel . . .

I feel very frustrated myself when I see you do that.

I'm bothered by . . .

If I describe what I see (pieces of paper on the floor) I have not said 'You've made a mess'. I have described what is affecting me. This is hard to do, but it is worth abandoning a 'Well done for clearing the floor' for something like 'The floor was covered in bits of paper, but now I don't see a single piece.' Tony Humphreys, in his book *A Different Kind of Teacher*, believes that since all communications are about the sender, it is far more accurate to use an 'I' statement. The examples he gives are 'I am impressed by your essay', and 'I like the colours you're wearing' (Humphreys 1995: 56). The 'I' message communicates something about the sender's perception, but leaves the recipient to evaluate for themselves.

'I' statements do not necessarily rule out the use of the word 'you' because this can also be part of descriptive praise. Using 'I' helps to focus my position. 'You' statements can probe and describe further. They are not so safe as 'I' statements because they can sometimes accuse the recipient. If we stick to description, however, we can use 'you'. I have organised the following examples into teacher comment and its conversion into possible pupil thoughts resulting from what the teacher says.

Teacher:	You organised the team, wrote out the league listing and kept the scores up to date.
Possible pupil self-talk:	I organised the team and kept everything up to date!
Teacher:	You understood the importance of having accurate co-ordinates in map-reading.
Possible pupil self-talk:	I can do co-ordinates and map-reading.
Teacher:	You still dived in and had a go. That's very difficult to do.
Possible pupil self-talk:	It was hard, but I did it!
Teacher:	You did that well ahead of time.
Possible pupil self-talk:	I'm really organised now.
Teacher:	Your diagram is clearly labelled and you set it out using the space well.
Possible pupil self-talk:	This is a good piece of work.

Faber and Mazlish (1980) advise, 'You're always on safe ground when you make a descriptive statement to a child about your own feelings.' Doing so puts no obligation on pupils to do anything but hear how we feel about something. They themselves will decide how, when and if they want to respond. If an adult continually tells children what to do, what to say, and judges that process, children can feel a tide of anger well up. Their psychological territory is invaded and they do not feel in control of things. How many teachers say, 'Think for yourselves!', then proceed to tell pupils what to think and how to think it? Pupils' resentment is sometimes inevitable as a means of self-protection and may show itself as sulking, passivity or grumbles (Humphreys 1996: 70). Giving descriptive praise when a pupil is simply getting on with working is positive. Often it is when children do something wrong that they get plenty of attention, a pattern going way back to being a toddler. Unexpected attention and praise is powerful if it contrasts with an adult's natural style of working with pupils.

Formative descriptive praise

It is not enough to praise pupils in a general way in order to motivate them because this is a lost opportunity. Much more can be done to give feedback that helps learning. Using specific descriptive praise can counteract the tendency some individuals have towards a higher than average need for approval. It is natural enough to want to be recognised and approved of, but this can lead to low tolerance of criticism when it does come (Bernard 1990: 128). The thinking of high approval-seekers tends to be 'I need people to approve of what I do' and 'It's awful to be criticised'. I can easily identify with this, and it is a commonly experienced thought-pattern for many teachers. An antidote, based on work by Ellis (1994), is to transmit the following message to pupils:

> Doing well can be satisfying, but all humans make mistakes, so approval may not come when it is most wanted. It is preferable to have approval, but not exactly life-threatening if it is absent. Mistakes are definitely things to be disliked, but need not become over-blown into imagined catastrophes. Concern is better than panic, and annoyance far better than anger.

If descriptive praise is to be formative it cannot be passive and there are two main ways to make it active. One way is for the teacher to develop dialogue about pupil self-assessment and teacher assessment. The other way is to encourage pupils to use positive self-talk. This means explaining to them how to repeat their better descriptions *to themselves*. Examples are saying things internally, such as 'I can write longer sentences, keep to the lines and use interesting words', 'I concentrated for a long time and it paid off'. How do we do that? By telling a pupil 'Say that to yourself inside your head, beginning with the word "I". You'll find it makes a difference.'

If we look at some of the pupil self-assessments from Chapter 5, we can see that pupils already describe to themselves without realising. Self-assessment is similar to descriptive self-praise when a pupil summarises, provided grades are not given as in 'I think we used the most effective ways of joining the materials together. There were really two options, glue or nails.' On other occasions pupils judge positively for themselves, as in 'We described our plans in great detail and it was good.' Even negative self-assessments provide an opportunity for a teacher to respond with positive descriptive praise. Note, in these examples, the teacher's description also includes encouragement (the teacher's tone of voice is intended to be one of interest and appreciation).

1   Deciding on an appropriate scale to draw a plan of a room
     Pupil's written self-assessment: We each said what scale we would like. I said

1 metre equals 10 centimetres. We tried this, but it didn't work, so we had to use a smaller scale.
Teacher's verbal response: You allowed each other to suggest ideas and were able to agree something to try out. When you realised it was not going to work, you used a smaller scale. You learned about the effect of your first decision and about changing this. So you know where the problems are in this task and you overcame them. That was good thinking.

2 Testing out paper folding
Pupil's written self-assessment: We tried to make a bridge, snooker-table, swords and a bird-table, but they didn't work.
Teacher's verbal response: You were very ambitious and it's a pity you didn't have more success. You found out about the weight of paper and difficulties joining paper together. Trying these things out was hard to do and I could see you all concentrating. We need to look at other ways to do this and improve the skills you have. Has anyone got an idea how to improve this if you had the chance again? What would you do?

3 Use of titles, labels and a key for the plan
Pupil's written self-assessment: We didn't use a key, but I wrote in block letters what some of the rooms were. I also wrote the measurements down the sides, what were the lengths of the walls, etc.
Teacher's verbal response: You made sure that your plan was drawn clearly enough for someone else to understand. There were labels on the walls themselves. You don't always need a key, but you might check that you know what one is. Ask your friends and tell me when you're sure about that. I'm really pleased by what you've managed to achieve. You've got a very interesting layout there. Do you see that?

These responses are preludes to pupil–teacher discussion. If positive praise is not to be passive, it is important to use the opportunity to ask pupils why and how their work might need changing. In dealing with pupil errors, a colleague who works in Canada explains formative descriptive praise like this:

Let's take writing about a tornado as an example. I'd look first for the good things about the writing. Does the student have a good grasp on what a tornado is? Great! Go with that, and I'd say, 'You've really got an understanding of tornadoes. I never really understood why they rotate counter-clockwise and you've helped me understand that. But, I think that some of the writing actually might be interfering with these good ideas that you have.' And then I'd go very specifically into one area or type of thing that the student could work on.

Or it might be that the understanding is not very good, but that the student is really interested in tornadoes, thinks they're really awesome. So, I'd say, 'I know that you are really taken by tornadoes, because I've seen you working really hard on this project and you've talked to me about it. But, somehow, your writing doesn't really reflect your excitement or your knowledge. So, let's tackle that so it shows.' My principle is not just that I start from a student's strength, though that is certainly true. But I try to let them know that I *value* their work, their interest, and their attempt to do what they're supposed to. That the work they've done is not for naught, but rather that we can make use of that work. And, that I know that they can do this.

(Professor of Education)

My colleague did not set out deliberately to practise descriptive praise, though she certainly understands it. Analysing these examples a little further, we can pick out some significant details. Her main principle is not just that she starts from a student's strength, but tries to show that she values their work. In doing this, she describes the tornado writing and manages to say what she herself never understood before. She then talks about errors as being *something getting in the way of what you can do.* In other words, 'You can do this, but we need to look at what is preventing you.' In the example of the student who is taken with tornadoes but does not know how to write, she includes the word 'because' as in 'because I've seen you working really hard on this project and you've talked to me about it'. Her approach is:

Do they understand? If so is there something I can describe about how I value what they're doing? If they don't understand, can I say something about how I value their interest? And can I suggest ways to reveal yet more through their writing as if the problems are just things that temporarily interfere?

She also points out things that her pupils took for granted. She notices that the pupil has been working hard or is absorbed by the subject and makes corrections and improvements sound possible. This ties in closely with my earlier point, that pupils need some time to build up credit for what they have tried to do before their errors can be pointed out. A number of high-achieving teachers have told me that throughout their lives they tended to be stubborn about not giving in to criticism. This is often a strong motivator of high achievers, but for most people requires stubborn determination in the face of negative comments. The ability to stick at things despite the odds is to be admired, but not all pupils can actually do this. There are other ways to motivate that still address the errors pupils make and difficulties they encounter.

When errors are plentiful, my Canadian colleague describes them as 'surface feature errors'.

If there were many errors, I'd have the student read the story aloud to me and we'd talk about the great features of the story . . . maybe relate it to other great writing the student has done, to confirm that this student has some really good ideas, can choose good descriptive words (or whatever) and we'd note some of those already in this story. Then, I'd look at the story with the student and let the student know where someone who did not hear him/her read the story would get distracted from the story by the use of non-conventional spelling, punctuation, grammar. I would remind the student that when we make our writing public, for others to read (whether they be classmates or a wider audience), if we don't use conventional notation then most readers may have difficulty reading the story in the way the student intended it. I'd say, 'Do you know how you paused right here? Well, without a comma/period your reader won't do that. They'll just read it like this . . . or else they'll get so distracted trying to figure out what words were intended (because of mis-spelling) that they lose track of the story or the description . . . '.

The student needs to understand both

- her/his strengths in the writing;
- why surface features like spelling and grammar matter.

The same might be true for a science report, as in 'Why do I have to use a chart for my data? Why can't I just write the numbers down?' The student needs to understand how the chart helps people compare those numbers much more easily. The chart is actually helping the reader understand just how powerful and exciting these data are. It's a matter of finding out what the student is doing well. And locating multiple instances of it, if possible. (Sometimes we have to go to previous work, so portfolios of student work are invaluable here.) So that the student really internalises that 'I can do some of this and do it really quite well'. Then, it's a matter of saying, 'So, given that all of this is going so well, what are we going to work on?' It might be that the student could identify this. Then, my role is to say, 'Great idea. What shall we do first?' or to say, 'You know, I think that is not too bad at all. It's coming along well. But, what about this over here?' That's my role as expert.

(Professor of Education)

What a difference when . . .

Enthusiasm in a teacher's voice can have a powerfully motivating effect, but it cannot be described exactly here. I assume it is a recognised quality. Directions given in the text of a stage play indicate intonation. Besides stage directions in brackets, such as *(goes over to window)*, we have *(said with excitement)*, or *(enthusiastically, as if sharing happiness)*. One of the most spontaneous descriptive phrases, used in a genuine and enthusiastic way, not sarcastically, is to say, 'What a difference when . . . '. Almost any description of 'What a difference when . . . ' could become sarcastic *(said with slight malice)*, or superficial *(blandly, as if of little importance*). Voice-tone and therefore the emotional level often transmit far more than words. The following examples are intended to be heard with the imagined stage direction (*as if sharing real pleasure in success*) or (*as if understanding what joy it means to the recipient*). They are examples gathered by chance and only a genuine interest in seeing a pupil progress will ensure spontaneity after initial rather studied practice of them. The shorthand for this is tuning in to how pupils feel and responding intuitively.

> What a difference when everything slots into place!
>
> What a difference now you have developed some skill in using a word-processor!
>
> What a difference from when you first started trying to read!
>
> It's so different now you take a little more care over organising your work!
>
> It's so much more exciting when you find out something you thought you didn't know!
>
> What a difference when you can do that up to speed!
>
> It's so different now it's a good habit.
>
> What a difference when you have a run of success!

The use, but not over-use, of this phrase is an exercise in sharing another's success, which is sometimes one of the hardest things for human beings to do.

> I have no difficulty letting these comments slide into the tone of voice of a pleased parent, at which point I realise I have probably sabotaged my comments. I have said 'What a difference when . . . ' as if achievement has rewarded *me* for past weeks of teaching. I would prefer to have retained a genuine feeling of sharing success with a pupil. When children reward me by achieving, my encouragement of their efforts may actually shift away from rewarding them. A voice can sound self-rewarding.
>
> (Primary-school teacher)

What is not often realised is that some individuals will not actually hear positive descriptive praise because they are predisposed to take notice of critical comments. This is very difficult to verify, but I have suspected it happens with several pupils. I have also found that trainee-teachers will ignore positive description if they heavily focus on what they have not yet achieved. It may be necessary to reiterate to a trainee that the class did not run riot, the pupils *were* mainly on-task, and the noise level *was* high, but tolerable. Suggestions for improvement can unfortunately imply what is wrong, rather than look to the future. I have found that some individuals are already rather disheartened before they begin, so they do not listen as well as they might and I misjudge the situation. It is harder to know how disheartened they are if we are in 'fix-it' mode, offering solutions instead of positive description of what we notice. Analysis of pupils' work can sometimes reveal that they wrote longer sentences, or paid attention to punctuation and spelling. They found interesting adjectives and they had some idea of the plot. They contributed to the session and answered questions. Closer examination of the teacher's lesson could reveal that they asked useful questions and, though things did not go smoothly, some quality work was produced. But will it? There is a strong inclination to look too hard at the blemishes, when we need to enlarge on what went right.

Self-praise and teachers

Descriptive self-praise for teachers can be an uncomfortable, rather less than British phenomenon. The profession is after all more used to criticism from quarters such as government, parents, local authorities and school inspectors. It is nothing new to hear a note of belligerence in the voices of people who seem to know better and are ready to point out that things are much worse than we ever wanted to believe. We can add to that the stress of unrealistic official demands on an almost daily basis, and, before long, things take a mournful turn. Some adults find that reading affirmations about themselves is a help, or repeating to themselves a list of positive qualities they know they have. I know teachers who will stand in front of a mirror and tell themselves about their uniqueness. There are other ways, as the following example illustrates. The context is that of a headteacher who was feeling very anxious about facing yet another school inspection. Adapting a reply from Albert Ellis posted on the Internet in November 1997, I suggested:

> You could pick your moment to say to yourself, 'I behave like a bright, mature person who has shown several times that she is capable of running a school. I keep getting to like you more for doing that.' Seems like a good idea? But it is not, because it can lead along the path of self-rating. Stick to saying 'I like the times when I'm coping better' rather than 'I like *me* for doing this job a bit better than I used to'. The self-rating game has implications for self-esteem, continually rating against the perceived demands of an inspection service, colleagues that you rate yourself against, that perfect headteacher in that imagined school somewhere. Worst of all is rating against your previous view of yourself. You know that getting worked up makes you function less effectively, but you need to see the sabotaging judgement of an attitude of continual self-rating. Learn self-praise that does not rate but describes some of the things you took for granted. Like saying to yourself 'I've already written some policies, and helped a member of staff who had difficulties. I daily manage parents and visitors. I've already written much of the school management plan and last year's was useful and clearly

understood by everyone. Parents want to send their children to your school, because the school is a supportive community and we all work together.' Why not shed the stressful baggage?

Unfortunately, school inspections, examinations, and consequent academic success and failure tend to encourage stressful self-rating. Making comparisons, even subconsciously, is not the same as doing well at that particular moment, or being rewarded for studying hard on this occasion. The real rating is actually done by a third party such as an examination board, interview panel or a team of inspectors. Judgements of this kind are unavoidable and may be necessary. Self-rating is what we might do in our mind as a result of transient success and failure. For the most part it may not seem to matter until something really big comes along such as an examination or a job interview. These are stressful items because we are judged and compared with a standard or another person. The self-rating game is a misunderstanding because it goes one unnecessary step further than saying 'I did this and I like what happened' (I got the qualification, the job, or had a successful inspection) or 'I did this and I did not like what happened' (I failed the test, did not get the job I wanted). The unnecessary self-rating step has been to say 'I did this and I'm therefore a better/worse person as a result.' Logically it is easy to see the nature of the error, but we seem to have an infinite capacity to camouflage ourselves against anything so logical. The feelings of being better or worse as a result of an examination can override logic. I feel worse, therefore I must *be* worse. Failing an examination can of course make me feel a failure and negatively affect my self-esteem. The question is for how long?

In teacher self-talk it is possible to describe all the things we have not managed to do, all the qualities we feel are missing and list every deadline not yet met. The list can grow and grow. These are used as evidence of failure. They have a demotivating, even paralysing, effect the more we take notice of them. An endless 'to do' list is actually a list of preferences dressed up as demands and there are two perceptions possible of such a list. The first perception is that I think the things I cross off the list are important now because I did them. The second perception is that crossed-off items do not count and only what is left can be allowed to loom large. I may even have my list on a computer, in which case deleted items on my list are no longer seen as being crossed off. Only the things still to do remain on screen. Chapter 8 describes this illusion in more detail.

KEY POINTS

- It is very hard for anyone to accept extravagant praise.
- Saying something is 'brilliant' simply does not carry enough information by itself.
- Deliberately practising the language of praise can lead to more spontaneous use of it.

- Only what remains ingrained as spontaneous and sincerely felt praise is effective in helping children to learn.
- Looking for specifically good things to praise can help a teacher begin to see more positive aspects of children's work.
- It may be possible for a teacher to experience a more positive day, through learning to practise descriptive praise and actually 'seeing the positive'.
- The word 'but' cancels what went before it.
- Pupils need to have time to hear and adjust to a positive description *before* they are ready for suggestions about improvement.
- There is nothing wrong with an initial reaction like 'Great!' or 'Good!' so long as it is immediately supplemented by specific description providing information.
- There is no point in becoming so apprehensive about avoiding judgements that we cease to be spontaneous.
- When I'm giving feedback is there something I can describe about how I value what they're doing? Is there anything I didn't know that they found out?
- Pupils' errors can be described as 'something getting in the way of what you can do'.
- When children reward me by achieving, my encouragement of their efforts may actually shift away from rewarding them. This subtlety of error is difficult to avoid, but not impossible.

Chapter 7

Nurturing success in children

We've had far too many pupils excluded for difficult behaviour and there has to be a way to do something about this. These children are not going to respond to praise and encouragement alone so there has to be a way to make them feel a bit special if we're going to move them in a more positive direction. They're a trial for most teachers and we're dealing here with things like bullying, anger, tantrums and disruption. We need to show we're having some impact on these children's lives or we're not doing our job.

(Middle-school teacher)

Positive aims of nurture groups

Preventing continual educational failure sounds ambitious because failure is almost impossible to avoid. Fortunately, that has never stopped teachers trying to help children whose experience of school is extremely negative. Changes in pupils' perceptions are almost always possible. My aim in this chapter is to describe ways in which difficult children might be nurtured in a small supportive group. The aim of 'nurturing' is for them to develop self-responsibility, credit themselves and function more effectively as learners. They do this partly by relating in a different way in a small group and partly by confronting their difficulties and devising ways to cope with them. This is not just a socialising process, but one very clearly focused on improving a pupil's ability to learn in a class. The strategies used in what are called 'nurture groups' have wider implications for mainstream classroom practice, and the effects of nurturing children in a small group are already well documented. Reports show that these groups have helped pupils to become more sociable, co-operative and amenable to learning (Bennathan and Boxall 1996: 10). The ideas I describe here are mainly derived from observing two teachers working with ten children who were thought to have missed vital areas of their early development. The names of both teachers have been changed to preserve confidentiality. I refer to them as Alison and Martin.

Nurture groups were set up in London in the 1970s by Marjorie Boxall, an educational psychologist. She set these up with her colleagues in response to concerns about rising school referrals and exclusions. Usually there were twelve children in a nurture group supported by a teacher and a helper. The principle underlying the London groups was that of responding to each child according to need, whether for comfort, like a baby, special attention, or concerned help for temper tantrums. A young child with a temper tantrum, for example, might be held until it was all over, or left to pummel a cushion. Boxall and her colleagues found that, as the children's needs were met, they began to develop greater trust and self-confidence. They became better organised and adapted positively to learning in a more formal setting (Bennathan and Boxall 1996: 10). An aim was to try to change pupils' perception of themselves, their peers, teachers and other adults. Many of the children in these groups came from disadvantaged backgrounds and it was felt they had missed being nurtured in their early years. Some children had parents who were mentally ill, and most children had experienced trauma of one kind or another. Almost all of them found it difficult to fit into the mainstream classroom and take part in activities. It was more usual for these children to spend their day disrupting lessons and creating tension in and out of the classroom.

Since those early days, nurture groups have proliferated and developed in different ways. Groups still retain an emphasis on play activities and support for experiences that the children might have missed. Playing games, making things, and experiencing a group enjoying being with one another have been found to be positive ways to foster relationships. There is also considerable emphasis on caring and sharing in groups. Many of the children who attend nurture groups are so driven by their needs that they are largely unaware of the effect their behaviour has on other people. The teacher and helper in these groups try to support children in such a way as to let them be listened to and taken seriously. They create opportunities to care for one another in the group. For some children, this is a first experience of being listened to with any seriousness by a group of people. If this sounds easy to do, experience has shown that it is nothing of the kind. Nurture groups are not an easy option for dealing with pupils' problems and steering them towards becoming effective learners. There are, for example, reports of very difficult nurture groups which actually reach a crescendo of bad behaviour before calming down and consolidating (Bennathan and Boxall 1996: 31). Anyone who sets up a nurture group needs to be sure of what they want to achieve and prepared to be tolerant of behavioural and emotional difficulties.

Nurture groups share several characteristics and I have been able to compile a summary of essentials for organising a group.

- There are never more than twelve children in a group, otherwise the group dynamic is insufficiently intimate.
- The group ideally needs two caring adults, preferably male and female so as to provide appropriate adult role models.

- The setting of the room itself is preferably a relaxed and informal one, giving the feeling of a welcoming atmosphere.
- The agenda in the group is the children's, not the teacher's.
- Teacher and helper are honest and humorous, and try to set good adult role models for children by behaving considerately towards each other. They share their humour, feelings and personal memories of fear, anger, joy and anxiety.
- Feelings and emotions are talked through rather than ignored.
- Anti-social and uncaring behaviour is confronted in terms of its effect on others.
- Ways of coping with the mainstream classroom difficulties are discussed and children in the group are encouraged to offer advice for others.

Apart from this, there are some reasonable assumptions that can be made about how groups will operate. Every opportunity is taken to value a child's contribution by ensuring that nobody interrupts them when it is their turn to speak. Children hold an object, sometimes a stuffed toy animal, when it is their turn and this signals who is to be heard, much as in other groups such as 'circle time' involving a whole class. Teachers use encouragement and descriptive praise (see Chapter 6) and children are made to feel accepted for who they are, not what they do. Teachers like Alison and Martin are skilful at bringing out children's feelings and private concerns rather than glossing over them. They speak to children in such a way as not to patronise them, using instead a voice-tone more appropriate to another adult than a child. In Alison and Martin's case, this was immediately noticeable, and at times I felt I was observing a group of adults rather than junior-school children. At other times, when children were upset and tearful, Alison would hold and cuddle them supportively.

No two nurture groups are exactly the same. Teachers work differently and there have been many developments from the first groups set up in London. Alison and Martin's approach in their middle school was to have the same group of 8–10-year-olds twice a week for an hour and a half over a period of eight or more weeks. Groups elsewhere have operated for eighteen months or more, running throughout a full day. Naturally, there are differences if the children are very young or about to leave school. Several groups have favoured the use of art materials, sand and jigsaw puzzles. Junior-school pupils will still enjoy scooping sand at a sensuous level (Bennathan and Boxall 1996: 30). Whatever the style, the teachers support and share experiences in a safe setting, suggest ideas, and participate in the roles needed by the children. One group reportedly gave children breakfast at 10 o'clock and found that it stabilised an otherwise highly disruptive atmosphere. If there is a common feature for all these groups, it is talking about situations that provoke trouble and angry feelings that children have. Alison and Martin found they could not slavishly follow previous models for nurture groups, so like many other teachers across the country, developed their own nurture style.

Group activities can be summarised:

- circle time – listening and sharing;
- short tasks leading to achievement and greater self-esteem;
- individual tasks addressing problems;
- co-operative games developing awareness of others;
- dice and board games, taking part and listening;
- cooking – co-operation, responsibility and sharing;
- art sessions – expressing feelings, working together.

The room in which Alison and Martin's group met was homely, with its cooker and sink. Suspended from the ceiling was a basket of soft toys, including rabbits, teddy bears and other animals. There was a small bookstand of appealing stories, a computer and a cupboard full of special needs resources used at other times. There were plastic counters, 'Multilink Cubes' and word cards. A long table dominated the centre of the room and the children sat around this. Other teachers might prefer to use a carpeted area with cushions for nurture groups, but Alison and Martin needed the table to play board games and write. There was a whiteboard in the room that Martin occasionally used.

Starting group sessions

All the group sessions I observed began with children washing their hands when they arrived. This was partly a symbolic act, but also sensible if food was to be eaten. Food, as Alison pointed out, is considered a powerful subliminal sign of bonding and giving, one often used by national children's organisations and other nurture groups. A previous older group in the school had ended their last nurture session by cooking biscuits and sharing them, even taking them round to their teachers. It is important in any session to include something eaten, even if it is just a sweet or a biscuit. Alison and Martin had originally introduced hand-washing because the room they used was full of new books and equipment. From that point onwards it had become a routine for every child who arrived and it persisted. Children needed to feel they were in a different group with different behaviour and different habits. Washing hands helped to set a different tone from their usual classroom behaviour. This done, the real starting point for nurture-group sessions was to gather around the table and for Alison to invite pupils to share concerns. These bordered on confession.

> ALISON: At the very first session, we will talk to the children about the fact that each of them has been chosen because they have some trouble in school, lessons, behaviour or something. On the occasions we've done this, the children immediately interrupt and tell us why they think they have been chosen. It's confessional. Somebody will say, 'I'm here because I can't do maths.' Another will say, 'I'm here because I keep

fighting the whole time.' That's what's happened on the last two occasions we've run a group and it's a very natural lead-in. The agenda must be the children's, and you have to be prepared to suspend any plans you might have had and go where the kids take you. Even if it's not where you want to go. We don't have any ground-rules other than those we usually have in school. So 'You can't be verbally or physically aggressive and you must not swear.' We do go on to talk about more specific behaviour in the group, and explain that everybody's got to have a hearing. Everybody's got to have an opportunity, and we say, 'Even if you don't agree with it you've got to accept it's their opinion.' We always have some symbol to hold when a child is talking. It used to be a fluffy toy, but we've used a wooden teddy as a talisman.

Alison admitted that she and Martin were fortunate that children wanted to confess so readily as soon as they were asked. It is important that the discussion arises from the pupils themselves, their feelings and their difficulties. A teacher-led agenda would not support and nurture, and would probably be counter-productive. The preferred style of running this group was to listen far more to children's feelings than intervene to give advice. Both teachers agreed that the start of a session is a time to resist and hear the concerns of pupils. An older group of pupils will usually want to talk about people and their feelings. The younger group I saw was happier to start talking about their love for pets and animals or their sadness about the loss of them. Alison thought that in the first session the younger group was not so ready to talk about their love for people or their losses. By the second session, the children were bringing along photographs of their pets, or if they had no pets they would bring in their well-loved teddy bears. What mattered was that they could talk about something important to them or to their families. They were never asked to bring anything in, but they often did so spontaneously.

> ALISON: It happened as well with the older group. They started bringing in particular mementoes that they wanted to share with the rest of the group. A lot of running a group is guesswork. It's the idea that we ourselves are prepared to share things like our fluffy toys [in this room] and trust you, so you might do the same. Then they want to share their favourite things with us.

Sharing did not stop there. Both Alison and Martin were prepared to share their experiences of loss, fear and anguish. Alison spoke about having to take her cat to the vet to be put down and how frightened she felt about it. As Alison put it,

> I don't think we can expect them to open up to us if we're not prepared to do the same. You have to be prepared to offer a bit about yourself don't you? It leads into discussing their response to adults generally. You're trying to get

them to understand that adults are not perfect, and don't have all the answers. Actually, they either think adults are perfect or that they themselves got the duff ones. Many of them are disappointed with their parents and the way they get treated as children.

I'm trying to give them the opportunity to respond differently. That can lead to self-responsibility. You cannot expect other people to behave responsibly if you don't start making an attempt to behave responsibly towards yourself and towards others. It's helpful if you've got a good memory for the snippets children and teachers let drop because you'll be able to use them later. It might be three weeks later that you use them, but it reassures them you were listening. Sometimes, you see, children will come to the group and say they've had a really good week and you say, 'But what about yesterday at playtime when you . . . ?' And at that point they don't know whether to deny it or confess it. It's not me being malicious. You have to approach it with a bit of humour as well without letting it go if it's bad behaviour. You're saying to them, 'That wasn't very clever that time, but you're not totally despicable are you? I don't reject you.'

A key message Alison tries to transmit is this:

> If you try to behave differently you'll find that it could change how people in school react to you.

Some children's only response to criticism or difficulty had previously been to lash out. There were some key issues that Alison wanted to address. The group looked at ways of improving work, their output of work, their behaviour with each other, their attitudes towards other people's hostility. In challenging this again, a gentle but firm adult tone of voice is helpful. With not a hint of accusation, more curiosity, Alison would gently say, 'But that's not true, is it? You're not being straight with me, are you?' In such moments of quiet confrontation Alison and Martin would wait silently, sometimes for a very long time, before a child responded. The rest of the group would wait silently too.

It was not unusual for the outwardly toughest of pupils to admit to not having many friends. Their anti-social behaviour seemed almost to provide a protection against loneliness, an alternative, negative way of making other pupils interact with them. A tough pupil admitting to loneliness can result in other pupils discussing how that person would disrupt in lessons, and drag other people into trouble. The group I saw would discuss how changing his behaviour might mean having more friends. One pupil talked about the fact that he knew that he was a liability and felt so lonely that he had had to run away from school. In the awkwardness of this moment, three pupils immediately volunteered to sit next to him in lessons and his face lit up with relief and happiness. He no longer runs off into the town shoplifting.

ALISON: You have to able to say the most unpleasant things to children in groups to confront their anti-social behaviour. And yet remain on good terms with them. You can end up slamming someone into the ground for appalling behaviour. Sometimes, the next day they literally fall down in the playground. Where do you think is the first place they come to for a sticking plaster?

Examples of enabling and challenging language

Skill in handling pupils' difficulties does not develop by accident. The nurture group had evolved from Alison and Martin's daily work in special needs, and their classroom language had evolved through long experience. In these other groups (which were not nurture groups), Alison would talk about targets for learning and the weekly reward, which was a trophy. She would also warn in advance, 'I'm going to test you on Friday next week to see if you know your 100 common words', an example of feedback expectancy (see Chapter 4). Where some teachers might reward pupils regardless of their achievement, Alison would be realistic and challenge pupils:

> Put your hands up those of you who don't think you would be up for the trophy this week! Kirsty, tell me why you think you're not up for it this week?
>
> So you're telling me you behaved badly because . . . ?

Kirsty would describe throwing peas in the school canteen, or shouting out answers in the maths lesson. Other pupils would confess to not being considerate and having a tantrum. 'I got chucked out of Geography', said one pupil. Alison had a back-up system called 'honourable mention' so the trophy was not the only reward that could be won. Several pupils had their best efforts to improve described.

There were control statements, such as Alison saying very firmly, 'I'm going to say it's David's turn now' and 'Tell Sandra I want to see her in ten minutes and tell her it's *not* optional'. In the nurture group itself, Alison and Martin would tune in to pupils' needs and feelings. They would do this with good humour, Alison beginning by saying, 'Did you hear my knees crick? I need to go to the garage for an oil change.' Classroom language that involved pupils included:

> I can see by your face, Peter, you forgot. Is that right?
>
> You look in a bit of a grumpy mood, Sarah. Are you feeling grumpy?
>
> You need to learn to point your eyeballs at the person who is talking in this group, don't you, Gary?
>
> You sound as if you felt very bored. Were you?

Lee's been waiting a long time to show us his holiday pictures. Now's your chance, Lee.

Do the ducks come when you call them? I've tasted chicken eggs, but I wondered if duck eggs tasted any different.

My cat would just lie around in the sun all day. What does yours do?

I think you already know a lot about understanding adults . . . tell me about . . .

Or advice would be offered:

If you hurt someone, you're actually hurting yourself in the end. Do you think that's true or not?

Alison would challenge and explain, particularly targeting feelings:

How did you feel about having your dog put down? Did it make you feel scared? I was really scared myself when my cat was put down.

Do you think it's OK to punch people? How does that make them feel?

You say you don't like your teacher, but how do you think she might feel about not wanting to teach pupils *she* doesn't like? It's tough luck for her, isn't it?

The reason you got told off was to stop making it worse for yourself in the end. Do you see that?

If you were adults, how do you think you would you solve this?

If you want him as a friend, you've got to treat him well. You let him and yourself down. You sat on your own at the side of the classroom, but we can't give you lessons on your own all week because it's too expensive. How do you feel about treating him better?

Bullying and name-calling were frequent issues:

Do you think it's right for you to be beaten up? Do you have a right to feel safe in the playground?

How do you think somebody feels who is bullied *every* day?

How is bullying someone for a joke different from bullying seriously?

It feels very uncomfortable when you have to admit to doing something bad. I don't think you're really being straight with me, David.

Why do you think James has more friends now?

It's one thing if you call somebody 'fatty' and they are not fat. But quite another if they are, because that really hurts them, doesn't it?

There were times when control statements were needed simply to keep the group on track. Intervention by both teachers was immediate:

You surprise me, David, because we're talking about something else . . .

Let's have something from you other than rudeness, Darren.

Chris. Don't go off at tangents because this is important.

I can't hear Adam, can I? I need to hear what he says and so do you.

I notice by the way you're sitting that you're not really bothered, Sarah. Can you give us your attention?

There were many supportive descriptions and comments like 'What a difference it makes when you find you can do that!', and 'Thank you for not shouting that. I've still got my hearing left.' The group became very serious about bullying and hurtful behaviour, humorous about events that could provide laughter. One pupil, for example, excitedly announced he was going to have a surprise party. Another pupil asked 'How do you already know that if it's supposed to be a surprise?'

The Mrs Miggins game

Games have a long track record in therapy and in teaching children life skills. The Victorians modelled 'Snakes and Ladders' as a teaching game, and 'inter-action' games in therapy groups are known to challenge and weld groups together. One 'question game' played by the nurture group with dice and a board was very powerful indeed. My involvement in it was to create questions and statements based on cognitive therapy. This development proved popular with pupils because of therapeutic 'advice' which came from a fictitious character I called Mrs Miggins. This was the only name I could think of at the time as being someone responsible for giving advice. Once we had developed Mrs Miggins and her advice, written on question cards, the game took off beyond our best expectations. Martin had originally seen a game similar to this board game played in a nurture group and he had already adapted it. The purpose of the game is to introduce questions in the safe setting of play. Martin explained:

The game is played on a board with about twenty coloured rectangles on it. These are each about the size of a playing card and designed to overlap each other roughly in the shape of a figure 8. There's a larger square in the centre to put all the counters on, some of which are little plastic animals. The idea is very simple. You throw a dice and if you land on a coloured square, you're asked a question from the cards of that same colour. We began by having questions on a list with a coloured dot next to them, but now we use coloured cards. In fact the questions repeat themselves and there's no significance whatever in the colour. We just pick up a question printed on that particular coloured card. We designed questions around places like the classroom, playground and corridors where children would be. Once the children have answered that question, they mark a coloured dot onto a piece of card which they each have with their name on it. That way, they have a record that they did something in the game. They mark this on their personal card with a coloured felt-tipped pen, the same colour as the question card. They take turns to play and are rewarded with a sweet from our very large jar. There are no winners or losers, just questions and a turn to answer them.

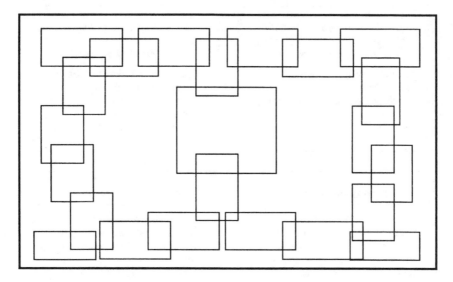

Figure 7.1 Design of the Mrs Miggins game board

As many children as possible need to have a role in the game. Roles include giving out counters, looking after the dice and the coloured felt-tipped pens. The child who has the felt-tipped pens, for example, is responsible for giving the right colour to the child who is answering so they can mark a personal record card with coloured dots. Another child arranges piles of coloured cards with questions on them, face downwards. There are small record cards with each child's name on to give out. The children's role includes moving each other's counters, though obviously they throw their own dice and answer the questions.

> MARTIN: I did wonder at one time whether we were giving children enough ideas to take away into the classroom. Some weeks we had not even

managed to complete questions because of what came up. I don't actually think that mattered too much because there were more valuable things going on. But sometimes they were so wrapped up in their own agenda I thought they would not really take anything much away with them. But because we had Mrs Miggins's advice they could look at the advice and read it, maybe take it away with them and remember it.

The following examples are a complete collection of the questions and advice from Mrs Miggins. They were printed for as many coloured cards as we wanted, with no regard for the fact that we were repeating the same Mrs Miggins advice. It was our very intention to repeat the advice over and over, based on what is known about the value of this in cognitive therapy.

I don't like my work when . . .

Mrs Miggins says:

You can't always like what you do. You can't like doing *everything* BUT you can like doing *something*.

I think people are bad when . . .

Mrs Miggins says:

A person's mistakes do not change their good qualities. It doesn't help to get upset over someone's behaviour that you yourself can't control.

I feel stupid when . . .

Mrs Miggins says:
Just because you feel stupid it doesn't mean you are. People are not brilliant or stupid all the time. Sometimes it takes a bit longer to understand things, that's all.

I get upset in class when . . .

Mrs Miggins says:
There may be a better way to look at things than thinking things *should* be different. Sometimes there is no reason why they *should* be.

I get really cross in class if the teacher . . .

Mrs Miggins says:

A lot of the time, you don't know it, but the teacher is trying to help and can't think how to. Teachers can't always do what you think they should do.

I really want to be liked by . . .

Mrs Miggins says:

Being liked by *someone* is possible. Being liked by *everybody* is NOT possible.

I don't think it's fair when . . .

Mrs Miggins says:

Why must people always treat you fairly? Why should people do what you want them to do all the time, and how does it help you to be angry over someone else's behaviour which you can't control?

If people call me names I . . .

Mrs Miggins says:

People can be hurtful, but it doesn't mean that if they call you a name it's *true*. We are all stupid sometimes but not stupid *all of the time*. It's just their nastiness. You need to know the difference between facts and name-calling.

I like to be praised for my work because . . .

Mrs Miggins says:

People do not always recognise when we do something well. Being praised and approved of does not always happen when we most want it to.

People do not *always* feel the same way because . . .

Mrs Miggins says:

People can like and dislike different things. Some people feel the same about different things. Other people do not, *so we had better not <u>IMAGINE</u> what we feel is going to be what <u>THEY</u> feel.*

I think people upset me most when . . .

Mrs Miggins says:

Other people can be nasty, but blaming them is ridiculous because we got upset by thinking that they *should* behave better. But they may not yet be able to.

People do not always smile and wave because . . .

Mrs Miggins says:

Just because people forget, or are in a different mood, it doesn't mean they don't like us. We forget that we are just the same ourselves *sometimes*.

I get really angry in lessons when . . .

Mrs Miggins says:

It's natural to feel anger, but it might not help to give in to it. You need a better way to get out of the situation in lessons.

I was worried when . . .

Mrs Miggins says:

It's normal to feel worried, but not a good idea to waste energy getting into a terrible panic if you can't do anything to change things right now.

Next time I feel upset I can . . .

Mrs Miggins says:

Try not to waste energy for too long after the first few minutes of allowing yourself to feel really angry. Try to think if it's because you believe things or people *should* be different when that's not possible.

If I behave badly, I feel . . .

Mrs Miggins says:

Everybody behaves badly sometimes, but it can upset people who might be trying to help and can't do that because of your behaviour. It's better to see you're getting yourself wound up and there could be better ways to get noticed in class.

If I could change something from the past . . .

Mrs Miggins says:

Changing the past is just a *silly* idea. Changing how you react next time is a *sensible* idea.

I feel worried in class if . . .

Mrs Miggins says:

You can feel worried anywhere at any time. Often there is not a very good reason to be worried, but a reason to be a bit concerned. Look for real evidence before you get too wound up about things.

I get angry when the work is . . .

Mrs Miggins says:

Sometimes work is boring or hard, but it's not impossible. If it's hard, that's sometimes how it is.

I hate it in class when . . .

Mrs Miggins says:

Some of the things you hate can teach you a great deal and build confidence. It's worth trying not to believe they *should* be any different.

I feel worried by things in class when . . .

Mrs Miggins says:

You are right to feel concern, but not right to worry. You may be thinking things that are not true about yourself. There may be a better explanation.

I feel scared in the playground when . . .

Mrs Miggins says:

It's right to feel scared sometimes, but being scared can make you aggressive. You need to watch yourself getting angry and try not to make yourself more scared.

I feel a bit stupid with friends
if . . .

Mrs Miggins says:

Your friends might not think you
are stupid just because you think
that. Better to think they will give
you a chance to be different next
time.

I feel stupid sometimes
because . . .

Mrs Miggins says:

We all have reasons to feel
stupid. It doesn't mean we're
completely stupid, just stupid
sometimes.

Next time I'm angry I will . . .

Mrs Miggins says:

Everybody gets angry. Try to
remember people try to protect
themselves by being angry. It
doesn't mean you need give in to
anger and get more upset than
you already are.

If there is one thing I would like to
improve in my personality it is . . .

Mrs Miggins says:

It's hard to change, but some
people find it useful if they
stubbornly refuse to give in to
difficulty. Then things change for
them. Set a personal target for the
week.

Next time anybody calls me
names . . .

Mrs Miggins says:

You need to say 'If you're trying to
upset me it worked and it's
hurtful.' Then remember that
name-calling is over the top and
therefore untrue. Just because you
got called a nasty name, it doesn't
mean it's true!

I feel really happy when . . .

Mrs Miggins says:

Little things can make you feel
happy. It's harder to feel happy
about good things happening to
other people, but possible.

Next time I think I'm stupid . . .

Mrs Miggins says:

You can realise that you are
name-calling about yourself. Just
because you feel stupid, it doesn't
mean you are. People are not
permanently stupid or brilliant.

I feel very down when . . .

Mrs Miggins says:

We all get times like that. There
may be another way to see things
other than thinking things *should* be
different. Sometimes there is no
reason why things *should* be any
different.

Next time, instead of trying to get noticed by being a pest . . .

Mrs Miggins says:

There are better ways to get noticed. You don't need to show off to get a laugh. You can get noticed for kindness too and trying to cope with not being the one who is the most important.

Next time I feel like wrecking a lesson . . .

Mrs Miggins says:

You can think how other people will feel if you stop them learning. Be really stubborn and refuse to give in. Then tell yourself you resisted showing off and that's hard – but you deserve to praise YOURSELF!

My work gets difficult in class when . . .

Mrs Miggins says:

Sometimes work gets difficult. Sometimes you just have to try longer to work it out by yourself.

I really hate it if people . . .

Mrs Miggins says:

You need to know a person's bad points are not everything. People have good qualities too, so hating them doesn't change things. It just makes you more angry if you can't see their good side.

I think I'm useless when . . .

Mrs Miggins says:

Thinking you're stupid is not the same as being stupid. You may think that, but remember people are not brilliant or stupid all the time.

Next time people call me names . . .

Mrs Miggins says:

People can hurt easily. Just because they called you a name it doesn't mean it's *true*. You need to know it is not a fact just because they said it.

I get angry if my friends . . .

Mrs Miggins says:

Sometimes friends do things they don't realise the effect of. They can't always do what you want.

If anyone praises my work, I feel . . .

Mrs Miggins says:

It's right to feel good about work. Doing things well is OK, but trying to be the best or brilliant is stressful. It's worth liking yourself even when you don't do so well.

It doesn't seem fair when . . .	I feel good about myself when . . .
Mrs Miggins says:	*Mrs Miggins says:*
Life isn't always fair. How does it help to get angry just because you discovered things are not always fair?	You can feel good if you tell yourself a list of things you already did. Like finishing work, saying 'Hello' to someone, listening carefully. They may not be big things, but you did them.

Children's responses to playing the Mrs Miggins game

It would be possible to put aside cards once used in the game and gradually reduce the remainder over a period of weeks. Martin and I were still against this because we felt it was important to repeat the same advice. One of the surprise moments came early on in the game when a girl's counter landed on a red square. Martin picked up a card on which was written, 'I really want to be liked by . . . '. Pausing only for a second, this pupil said, 'I really want to be liked by everybody in the school.' Mrs Miggins's advice is *'Being liked by someone is possible. Being liked by everybody is not possible.'* 'But how does Mrs Miggins know what I'm thinking?' questioned this pupil. Two or three more questions later, the children were quite convinced that Mrs Miggins was a real person who could read their thoughts. Martin quietly remarked, 'Well, I suppose she must be a bit special.'

> ALISON: I was trying to explain the game to a visitor and the children simply took over. It was amusing because they started explaining about Mrs Miggins. And one of them said, 'She's magic you know. She knows what we're thinking. She's a magic woman.' And somebody else said, 'She's right clever', and they are convinced she is a real person who has extra-sensory powers.

The children soon become adept at running the game themselves, with very little prompting. One child even acted as 'reader' for all the others and looked after the piles of coloured question cards. By the third session, the pupils were so keen to play the game that they took over the organisation completely and gave out materials. There was one important exception to this. Alison and Martin both intervened to use the game as a vehicle for discussing behaviour, problems and co-operation. A tacitly understood rule was that the teachers can do this and it is expected that they will intervene. Alison, in particular, was skilful at not letting things go, but pursuing them with questions such as 'But why would that not be a good idea?', 'Why do you think that?', 'Yes, but why? Give me a reason' and 'What could you do next time that would be better?'

When I visited the group towards the end of their series of sessions I was asked what Mrs Miggins looked like, so real had she become for the children. I improvised and said that I thought she was a grey-haired granny who was very wise and chuckled to herself a great deal. In our experience, the game was a remarkable success because it offered strategies for change as well as opportunities to discuss behaviour and academic progress. It also had the advantage that if the discussion was proving to be too uncomfortable, we could announce that it was someone's turn and continue the game. Nothing is a substitute for skilful questioning by Alison and Martin, but there is sufficient material in Mrs Miggins's questions to apply endlessly to school and home situations.

We wanted to promote transfer to the mainstream classroom through the game. It is a game that can be played elsewhere, but one of the developments we liked was for the children in the nurture group to say what their favourite Mrs Miggins advice had been. The aim of this was to revisit the advice as being something to take away for the rest of the day or week. Martin wrote up his 'Mrs Miggins's thoughts for today' on the whiteboard. One boy, for example, was able to recite verbatim Mrs Miggins's advice about anger. There is no sure-fire way of proving that transfer to the mainstream classroom occurs and that children remember the suggestions and strategies for change. We were convinced that transfer was possible. The cards for the game, for example, are biased in intention towards encouraging self-responsibility, so could easily be woven into daily practice. There are many chances for giving feedback about progress and using the Mrs Miggins ideas to boost confidence and reduce anxiety. An obvious invitation to classroom discussion is to say to a pupil, 'What do you think Mrs Miggins would say?' In the wrong hands this could be detrimental, especially if Mrs Miggins became a nagging matriarch, someone 'out to get you'. Handled with sensitivity, Mrs Miggins's advice is useful in any situation where feedback is given. We imagine its use in a mainstream classroom where it has been established that Mrs Miggins is a friendly, wise, humorous and popular figure.

Alison and Martin involved other staff from the school. Some staff already use the 'circle-time' approach where the class sits in a circle and discusses what makes them angry or happy in school. A full class of pupils does not lend itself to nurture, in the way a small group does, so there are likely to be differences of ethos. There is a much more convincing reason to involve staff, however, as Alison explained:

> The more people you can get involved, by stealth, the more you'll change the school ethos for the better. It's like good classroom practice, but taken a bit further, isn't it? It is important to be able to support children without going against other staff and colluding. Otherwise the member of staff will ask a child to get out their books and they'll refuse. That's not much good.

Martin had the additional idea of each class spending a couple of minutes at the start of the day choosing a much-enlarged Mrs Miggins card to display with advice. There are wittier possibilities, such as the Mrs Miggins Award for Dealing with Anger, or the Mrs Miggins Save Wasting my Emotional Energy Award. There are also possibilities for school assemblies based on real events happening in the school. None of this is straightforward, but could be inventive, creative and fun.

There are different effects as a result of group size and setting, as Martin pointed out:

> One of the difficulties in transferring anything is that children seem to have a preconceived idea of how they behave in class and how they behave in a nurture group. They treat it differently. This idea of 'who I am' in a classroom comes from somewhere. In a nurture group you're not continually pushing towards academic things they can't do. Sometimes you have to withdraw things they find difficult academically so you can 'nurture' some success. You are going to get a positive reaction behaviourally and socially through a nurture group. You should also get some positive reaction academically. We haven't actually tested this, but the children and staff say this happens. I think there's a need for a top-up after a few weeks away from the group. And for this you can't have a timetable set in stone or it won't happen.

Another positive feature of the Mrs Miggins game is that it is a playful way of learning to reframe events. Learning to see setbacks in a more positive light has already been described in Chapter 2 as 'reframing', though this is only a part of the story for children with special needs. There are many pupils who would find reframing very hard to do unless it began in a game. There are gaps in their early experience which warrant a different approach. Reframing requires pupils to be willing to trust their teacher and be biddable. The technique of reframing, it may be remembered, is not a way to avoid realities and failures, but to recognise them, overturn them and find a more healthy perception. This is a very valuable technique to learn because it short-circuits the tendency to prolong gloomy thoughts about failure. Unfortunately, some children are not biddable, so it is difficult to sustain their attention long enough to teach them how to reframe and support themselves.

Mrs Miggins's advice can be incorporated as feedback in the following circumstances:

- when inviting and responding to questions;
- in a class forum such as circle time;
- when writing comments when marking work;
- on a notice-board or bulletin-board;
- when counselling an individual pupil;
- in school assemblies;
- when talking with parents and colleagues.

A necessary caution repeated throughout these chapters is that nothing works better than spontaneity in using these ideas. We need to move from studied practice of them to spontaneity. It makes a difference when the opportunity presents itself by chance and these ideas are used in a real situation. It is so different from 'trying to be spontaneous' or manipulating events. Meanwhile, the imagination and humour of a fictitious, granny-like Mrs Miggins are undeniably addictive in a nurture group. It is here that the game can provide a relatively safe way of identifying and coming to terms with uncomfortable feelings.

KEY POINTS

- What matters in a nurture group is that pupils can talk about something important to them.
- A key message transmitted to groups is 'If you try to behave differently you'll find that it could change how people in school react to you'.
- It is important to include something eaten, even if that is just a sweet or a biscuit.
- The agenda in the group is the children's, not the teacher's.
- Feelings and emotions are talked through rather than ignored.
- Anti-social and uncaring behaviour is confronted in terms of its effect on others.
- Ways of coping with the mainstream classroom difficulties are discussed and children in the group are encouraged to offer advice for others.
- As many children as possible need to have a role in the Mrs Miggins game.
- The more people you can get involved, by stealth, the more you'll change the school ethos for the better (Alison).

Chapter 8

Stress reduction for teachers

The person least likely to listen to advice on coping with stress is someone who is already working under stress. Stress is humourless. I have never subscribed to the view that teachers can simply think their way out of stressful situations by laughing at them, 'being positive' or taking deep breaths in and out of a paper bag. Unreasonable workloads, demands for planning, disruption, interruptions, deadlines, assessments and school inspections are very real. These feel stressful because they are stressful. Dealing with disruptive pupils on a daily basis is particularly stressful, as is coping with occasional pupil or parent confrontations, and keeping calm in the face of provocation. In the background there may also be stress at home, or the stress of illness. Managing a whole class at the same time as thinking what to do next splits the mind in several directions, as can the continual watchfulness necessary to check that pupils are on-task.

A visitor from another planet would immediately notice that schools are places where the best-laid plans go wrong. There are numerous interruptions to thought and action simply because a school has children and teachers in it. If stress is in the mind, then one way to minimise it is to try not to split a teacher's attention with too many different claims at once. Flexibility and adaptability are almost always at a premium in any school, but there are unnecessary invasions of mind in some of them. In one school I visited there were two stress-prevention notices in the staffroom.

Nobody may interrupt any lesson during the first 20 minutes.

This phone must not be used to create a problem for anyone else.

Neither of these rules is necessary in some schools, but in others there are numerous stressful interruptions during the important start of lessons. Teachers and pupils lose the thread of what they are trying to do, and there is a continual recap of what has already been explained. Restarts and further interruptions prevail. In other schools where there are very few interruptions, the difference is noticeable.

My aim in this chapter is to indicate some ways in which we might minimise adverse reactions to stress. I do not intend to deal with the more obvious recommendations, such as taking a long soak in the bath, meditating, having a good social life, listening to music, gardening, hobbies and physical exercise. There are well-known benefits to be had from adjusting lifestyle to create oases of enjoyable distraction or alternatives to a mind-set of 24-hour-a-day education. Avoiding stressful circumstances is not always possible, and in some circumstances stress may actually enhance performance. My concern here is with how teachers minimise but do not eradicate stress by taking a healthier view of the apparent demands made on them. There is no doubt that several situations in teaching can lead to what we commonly refer to as 'stress'. The oddity is that the same events can produce anger, emotional arousal and physiological sensations in one person while another experiences nothing of the kind. The logic that follows is that it is not the event itself, but the state of mind produced that makes the difference (Abrams and Ellis 1994: 40). Stress is not events themselves, but our beliefs and reactions to those events.

Stress as a reaction to disruption, interruptions and deadlines is usual. Deadlines, because they pressurise against the clock, are frequent sources of stress for many teachers, as are any competing demands on time and workload. Some realities concerning deadlines are:

- I can do this, or give it to someone else to do, or it does not get done. Anything else is just fantasy.
- That this MUST be done by Friday actually means there is the strongest possible PREFERENCE that it is done by Friday. It probably will be done by Friday because it's important. There are consequences for not meeting this deadline, but it is still a strong preference, not a life-or-death demand.
- A 'things-to-do' list with no fixed limit can grow to the point where everything on the list MUST be done perfectly or I am not coping. The reality is that picking three things from the list and doing one of them is about all that is actually possible. Not everything on the list requires the same saintly attention.
- Like trying to cross the road, there actually ARE gaps in the traffic and it is important to take advantage of them. Pressure and demands come in traffic bottlenecks, but may not be perceived that way at the time.
- After hearing three questions, deciding on three tasks or knowing of three deadlines, the mind's memory banks are probably full.
- Self-rating and comparison with others who seem better able to cope with deadlines are unhelpful.

The controversial statement I have made here is the one about deadlines being preferences. Deadlines are surely deadlines? The deadline *must* be kept or it is not a deadline. If the plane takes off and if I'm not on board then I've missed it. Nobody could deny that, but not all deadlines are like planes taking off. There are other perceptions for meeting a deadline. Meeting a deadline is obviously a good idea, but anticipating a deadline, even thinking it means that we need to act immediately can actually produce stress for other people.

We agreed as a staff that pupils' reports would be completed in six weeks. My deputy returned them to me completed after a week. Done, finished and immaculate. 'For God's sake', I said, 'don't let the rest of the staff know you finished them, Debbie. You'll put tremendous pressure on them if you do.' She couldn't understand why some of the staff would feel guilty about not even having started. She'd leapt in and done them all ready for me to read. And that's how Debbie is because she can't bear things hanging over her so she finishes them early. Another member of staff will say, 'Dave, I know these reports are supposed to be finished by Friday, but are you really going to look at all of them before Monday?' She'll stretch my deadline to Tuesday because that's how she works. Written last minute and handed in on Monday. They'll all be done before I could get round to reading them. Debbie's a bit of a perfectionist who would probably be stressed if she didn't do them immediately.

(Primary-school headteacher)

As one teacher put it, 'Failure in others I can cope with. It's genius and sainthood in a teacher that I find more difficult to handle.' This is almost an argument for not doing things stunningly well, in case we threaten colleagues, except of course that we have no control over how others will see things. We may think we can influence the perceptions of others, but this is something of an illusion. Teachers who do things stunningly well are not going to be satisfied with accepting less from themselves, so are unlikely to reduce the time and effort they put in. There are echoes here of the sainthood threat residing once again within the self-rating game. Closer scrutiny reveals that stress invariably comes from adversely comparing and rating – a theory which, if it is true, is difficult for many teachers to take advantage of. The fact of the matter is that teachers often *do* feel inadequate compared with an apparently highly competent colleague. The threat to others posed by beating a deadline in a week instead of six is very real for some teachers if they do not recognise self-rating and comparison as being stress-makers. Perceptions differ, so one teacher may be impressed that a deadline has been short-circuited, while another is threatened by such perfectionism. Yet another cries, 'Get a life, why don't you!' because saints are too difficult to live with.

Recognising and avoiding stress in teaching

If a bus driver has twelve trips to do in a day, the job schedule is finite. A bus driver will not do thirteen trips because the bus company schedule has already finished. Teaching is stressful because the job does not define itself. Therefore it is open to irrational definitions. Irrational definitions are most likely to lead to 'self-rating' because, however much effort is put in, the effort will not consistently be perceived as being enough, good enough or the best that can be achieved. Sometimes it will be the best, but not *consistently* the best, because that is irrational and unsustainable. The buzz of self-approval gained from working flat out until something is the best is enough to keep some teachers stressfully engaged. An alternative view comes from a first-school headteacher who is familiar with the problem of an undefined workload:

> How do you walk away from the job? It's always half-finished. If you can't set realistic boundaries, you'll live with stress. Get better at defining the job. There's no need to limit the job, but there is a great need to set realistic timescales and say 'No' when you have to.

An implied piece of wisdom in this is to stop trying to finish a job that is already defined as unfinishable. Under the Yes-I-know-all-that-but principle, we can know that the job is always half finished, BUT it does not necessarily feel that way, so we carry on. We may even go so far as to reject the *always* half-finished from our definition of the job, but we will still carry on trying to finish the unfinishable. Sometimes there is a sense of having finished the day. But do we then continue to live as if the job that we so badly defined in the first place must somehow be finished and *can* be finished in the longer term? We have gone down another cul-de-sac of irrational thought and created a demanding rule that says, 'I *must* finish this and finish it well at all times or I am not coping with the job.' The demand leads to a self-rating of failure. Rules, especially self-imposed rules, can be stressful because they are general rules that do not always fit real situations. For example, a rule about school uniform or the wearing of jewellery at school (apart from safety issues) may be necessary, but will cause stress for some teachers if they insist absolutely on sticking to the rules.

> Many of my staff don't want to climb down and bend the rules. But holding the line about jewellery in the culture my kids come from is really very difficult. So I ask myself, 'Is it worth hanging on to this come what may and till death us do part?' You look at your principles to see what's there. I might find I get really worried if they're late, or I really insist they have this or that or they don't ever do this! Now with all that stuff, you look closely at your principles and say to yourself, 'Do I really need to hold the line on this every time *always*? Or is it something that's to do with my need for security or maybe my upbringing that's doing this?' You may find if you look closer that you're much better off compromising or even letting go of some rules now and again to avoid stress. You were holding on to the rule, but you weren't holding on to the best course of action, were you? It was probably wiser to let it go, but you didn't realise that because you were angry about it and got fixated on the rule.
>
> (Primary-school headteacher)

If parents take one view, and teachers in a school take another, it is a tremendous arrogance to think that the parents' views will easily be changed. This is to assume powers that do not exist. Parents' views may change, but they may not.

Compromise is inevitable if parents' feelings are to be validated and their co-operation encouraged.

Suppose my rule is 'Pupils should not answer back, swear or be rude in my presence'. As a teacher, I will feel threatened if a pupil who swears or is rude challenges my fixed beliefs about status. As Rogers (1992) explains, in an ideal world pupils should not answer back and be rude, and should not swear. Pupils maybe would not do so if they had better social skills or did not use attention-seeking behaviour in order to gain a sense of importance in a group. But they do. If my rule is 'They *must* respect me' and I am inflexible about it, sooner or later my self-esteem is going to be threatened. An over-rigid view of status, and insistence on respect when there are threats to authority create self-sabotaging outcomes if we let them. There is a considerable difference between a belief that leads us to say, 'I can't stand it!' and saying, 'OK, it's annoying, but not the end of the world when they do that' (Rogers 1992: 15). Believing that a pupil should respect teachers is different from desiring or wanting them to do so. Desiring or wanting them to be respectful means I will settle for respect most of the time, but not in all possible circumstances.

If a teacher draws the line somewhere (there is always a line to draw somewhere) there is a cost to doing so. The questions to ask are:

- Why do I stand so strongly by these principles?
- Why do I believe what I believe?
- Is what I believe worth sticking to, come hell or high water, anyway?
- What is likely to be the cost to me in emotional terms of actually sticking to this?

Stress is usually experienced as worry, but rarely as one worry even if one major event or threat seems to dominate the mind. Most likely, stress is a series or a combination of responses to events and factors. Stress as worry comes in infinite forms and can accumulate as several stress-provoking events naturally arise. An example is stress commonly triggered by change of any kind. Changes of job, house, relationship or states of health are likely to cause stress for many people. Few would deny that waiting for the results of medical tests or awaiting the outcome of an interview is stressful, but even the imagined effects of change can cause stress. A teacher who imagines that redundancy is always around the corner, when it is unlikely, is probably going to experience unnecessary stress.

Teaching is first and foremost a public occupation where the teacher is on show for most of the time. Uninformed criticisms from the public and almost impossible demands made on teachers are experienced in nearly every country in the world. Teachers are blamed for not coming up with the goods. Across the globe there is nothing new about teaching being an over-criticised profession. Teaching has a fluctuating status in the public consciousness as the ills of society are blamed on the quality of education. Teachers work publicly in year groups, in staff meetings with colleagues and parents, frequently functioning in the public eye. In primary education, for example, there is nothing more stressful for some teachers than organising a class assembly. Each class in a primary school takes turns to do an assembly seen by others in a public setting. Teachers can find this stressful if they know it is not their strong point, because stress can result from being seen to do things in public we do not particularly want to do. Either we do them (and we may become better at them through saturation), or we take steps to avoid them. Teaching, like it or not, is competitive, and it is quite likely for a teacher to be surrounded by artistic colleagues, and not be artistic, or by mathematical colleagues, and not be mathematical.

> I'm using simple examples here to make a point. Somebody can do a stunning assembly, which puts massive pressure on everybody else to do the same. It may be that administratively you are not very strong and somebody else produces immaculate and accurate documents, and that's another pressure. You're part of a team, but it's so often competitive when it needn't be. There is unfair competitive pressure because of the criticism from the media and parents. Read it and believe it. Attainment targets and professional expectations have a lot of stress attached to them whether you like it or not.
>
> (Headteacher)

We experience stress as being the effect on us of strongly irritating and difficult events. Mrs Miggins, from the previous chapter, would probably say, 'A stress-free life is *impossible*. Coping with stress is possible, but not *always* possible in *every* situation by *everyone all the time*.' Lack of support and recognition from others can be stressful, but most probably not living up to our expectations of ourselves is the most stressful of all.

Doing well, doing badly and perfectionism

> 'I learned two things early on,' my sister said. 'The first is don't blame people for being the way they are.'
> 'What's the second?' I said. She smiled.
> 'If they're really stupid,' she said, 'go ahead and blame them. It's a really simple philosophy', she added.
>
> (Andreas 1996)

This extract from a book of stories by Brian Andreas captures the essentially human trait of doing almost exactly the opposite of what we want to believe is good for us. I have already mentioned the self-rating that teachers do which sabotages them (chapters 3, 5 and 6). I described examples in these chapters as culs-de-sac of thought. We are led down them unless we can see them for what they are. I freely admit that I still find myself led down one or other thought-trap before I realise what has happened, but I know that the most twisted of these is the one that says, 'I *should* recognise *all* these thought-traps by now'. So it is with teachers accepting themselves unconditionally whether they do well or badly, not rating themselves, but merely rating their acts and performance. An example of a thought-trap comes from a middle-school teacher who has tried to talk up her achievements.

> I realised I could tell myself that I had proved more than once that I teach well. We had done a project on 'electricity' and the test results from exams were high. We had a wonderful wall-display and I got lots of comments about it being outstanding. Then there was all the effort I put into running the computer club and making sure everything worked just fine. I got on well with other staff and children liked me. I knew that I could explain things clearly and get a high standard of writing from children. So on a scale of one to ten I must rate as being at least an eight or nine. I could say, 'Yeah. I'm better than I was at teaching and I like myself all the more for what I've achieved. I can do lots of things that other teachers can't do.' 'Yes, I feel much better now I know I'm a good teacher, a nine rather than a two like I used to be.'

The thought-trap exemplified in this story is the self-sabotaging one of putting a label on achievement. Not even school inspectors can rate more than the lesson they actually see. The trouble is that a rating for a lesson becomes a rating for a teacher unless the folly of self-rating is understood for the fantasy it is. It is far less damaging to say, 'I like the things I achieve and when the times are good I like them too.' In old-fashioned rating terms, some days in some lessons I rated a nine, but today this lesson was a definite two. At least that rates a specific lesson, but why rate it? Self-esteem takes a dive if it involves the fiction of consistent self-worth. I could just enjoy doing one or two things that I do well instead of self-rating. Positive self-rating is certainly less stressful than negative self-rating, and can lead to a temporary feeling of boosted self-esteem. Self-rating can be very motivating and give a pleasurable feeling of delight in the praise often experienced from others. But it is damaging all the same because it rates, and therefore sets us up for a fall, especially if stressful events come along soon after a positive self-rating. There is a strong connection between what this middle-school teacher says and a quotation about disputing feelings of worthlessness when events take a turn for the worse.

> *Question*: Is it true that I am an inadequate, worthless person if I do not handle stressful conditions well and even make them worse?
> *Answer*: No, I am a person who may well be acting inadequately at this time in this respect but I am never a totally worthless (or good) person, just a fallible human who is doing my best to cope with difficult conditions.
> (Abrams and Ellis 1994: 47)

My question and answer would be:

> *Question*: Is it true that everyone who knows my lesson was rated by inspectors as a Grade 2 will think that I'm a Grade 2 teacher?
>
> *Answer*: Not everyone. Some will because they don't understand self-rating, but your real problem might be that it worries you to think that they do. You cannot influence their perceptions and if you need the security of a higher grade, you don't understand the rating game either. You were rated a 2 this time, for this lesson. You're not a worthless or good person if you got a 1 or a 71. You got a Grade 2 this time. That's all.

The disadvantages of self-rating can be enormous, because any significant lapse in high ability or performance is stressfully experienced as failure. As Ellis (1998a) puts it, 'Any significant lapse and you immediately down yourself. And then, when you do down yourself, you tend to lapse more. A truly vicious circle!' As he goes on to say, even if we have enormous talents and abilities, in order to rate ourselves and minimise our stress we have to display them virtually all the time. If we rate ourselves and succeed in giving ourselves a superior rating, we can be deluded into thinking we really are superior. The sense of self-esteem is then about as false as it ever gets. It is self-esteem that is so fragile the slightest knock will shatter it. Ellis also warns against insisting on rating ourselves as good or bad because of the natural tendency to focus on defects and failings rather than successes. We are likely to preoccupy ourselves with sidetracking goals.

One of these unfortunate sidetracking goals is that of trying to 'be the best'. Whatever would happen if we all wanted to be the best? This is a particularly stress-producing goal because it demands self-rating even to believe we can become the best. Imagine a race to the finishing post. If there is a runner who is way out in front, and outstandingly good, I will find it difficult to improve my pace. I can increase my pace if I am quite close to the runner ahead of me, but comparing myself with one who is miles in front is a waste of energy. I will settle for a good, natural pace and run as well as I can. I will not be the best, but I will do a good time and improve on the previous effort if I can. If the race is to become a high-quality teacher, then the finishing post does not even exist. High quality is a stretchable concept and never defined unless we define it ourselves.

A perfectionist can argue this rather differently:

> I can understand that it doesn't matter what other people think (and I don't think this is my problem), but I can't help wanting to be a Grade 1 teacher FOR MYSELF. Looking in the mirror, if I were the only person in the world who knew my grade, I would *still* want to be a Grade 1, wouldn't I? Why? Because otherwise, I've left something out, wasted some time somewhere along the line. I've put myself forward for something that I thought I could do really well and I wanted to do well. Then I feel I haven't a clue when it goes wrong. I suppose I only want to do something if it's fairly risk-free and I know I can do it.
>
> (Teacher)

What might the mirror say back?

> If you deny how you feel, all that happens is you invalidate real feelings about feeling clueless when you wanted to be a Grade 1 for yourself. Feeling clueless, though, is definitely not the same thing as being clueless. Even if you understand this, there's a gap between knowing it's true in your head and feeling it in your guts, which is what's known as the gut gap. Grade 1 is a fiction which is self-sabotaging and prevents you realising that someone passed you a violin and told you to learn how to play it. But you told yourself, 'Don't play in public until you can play the Mendelssohn Violin Concerto.' In reality, playing 'Three Blind Mice' or 'Twinkle Twinkle Little Star' would do for a start. You could even try praising yourself for the effort you've put in. As for the gut gap, mind has to hit muscle before anything will happen.

And the perfectionist replies:

> Closing the gap? It's all very well to say that, but how do I close the gut gap? My head knows it is being unrealistic to play the Mendelssohn Violin Concerto, but how do I content myself playing 'Three Blind Mice'?

The mirror replies:

> The answer to this is very plain. If you were to try to close the gap yourself, by definition it would not exist as a gut gap. It is not necessary to do anything about the gap once you realise that self-rating is illogical. The gut gap is how things actually are until emotions catch up with new thoughts. The gap is not something to be closed prematurely because mind hits muscle at its own pace and it may take days or weeks before the gap closes by itself. In teaching, the fiction of being a Grade 1 teacher is healthily undermined by having a good, not so good, rewarding, disappointing, easy, frustrating, elating and difficult week.

Some stress-busting ideas

The rating game has existed for a long time in the shape of examinations, school inspections, league tables and career profiles. Reports of the emotional upset these can cause have spread as much by word of mouth as through 1990s reports in *The Times Educational Supplement* of the rise in stress-related illness. Some of the associated stress can be attributed to the fact that rating in the United Kingdom of the 1990s has been a public naming and shaming activity. What was meant to be an inspector's snapshot of a school's activities soon turned into a global rating, often regardless of the circumstances. If this shows anything, it is that rating and judging are unavoidably stressful and threatening. Rating and judging are not going to go away, but it follows that it is not what happens, but what we believe about what happens, that makes the difference.

The following stress-busting ideas have resulted from interviews and a synthesis of ideas I have found to work over a period of time. These cover school inspections, pupils who refuse to co-operate, financial worries and pressurised deadlines, all of which are stressful. Anger, leading to stress, is often an invasion of feelings about events and actions that we feel we cannot control when we want to. The job of teaching does not lend itself to total control, but a number of teachers who experience stress experience it because they feel they must be in control more than they actually are. They want to be in three places at once or control other people's wills. Two questions are important to ask in any of the examples I have chosen:

- Is this within my control?
- How well do I know myself?

The two examples I have decided to explore first are school inspections and a deficit school or department budget. Both can mix emotional responses with the stark reality, and the result is stress.

> I have this school inspection coming up next term. Emotionally, I worry about whether the inspectors will perceive the school in the way I want them to. I know I have no influence over that, but it doesn't stop me feeling that I have. If we had done nothing to prepare for it, I would be stressed. No school is going to ignore preparation completely. So we've already done several things. We're in a situation that will make us prepare far more evidence than we might have done and we can make sure we don't focus on what's missing, but on what's been done so far. It's so easy to forget what's already been done. Those are the bits within our control. It doesn't mean we ignore what's still left, but don't ignore what we already prepared as if it doesn't count. We can revise policies, display work and make sure planning is on paper. We can share frustrations, mend a few fences, but if we have done what we can in the time we've got, then that's it. That's it and the rest is outside our control. When the inspectors arrive, I can drag their noses towards things I'd like them to see, but I have no control over my teachers' abilities, the way children react on the day or whether it will rain buckets. I'd like the sun to shine, but I think I'll still survive if it doesn't.
>
> (Primary-school headteacher)

The message of this stress-busting idea is that it is worth asking these questions:
- Is reality refusing to meet my ideas?
- Do I not only want to control my world, but probably the galaxy of the Milky Way as well?

Even if I think that something is within my control, that does not mean I *must* be able to control it. There is a daily failure quotient allowed.

Analysis

When reality refuses to meet our demand of being in control, what happens? We blame reality.

- Those kids make me so furious.
- He made me so angry when he refused.
- This makes me so cross.
- It's their fault.
- It's his fault.
- That should not have happened.

By blaming others, you remove any power you have to take control of your stress. You then have to rely on the outside world to change before you can change (Bernard 1990: 70).

The second aspect of stress busting is illustrated by the following interview extract about coping with a school or department budget. One person's perception here is different from another's:

ME: You said that your school budget is shot to pieces this year, which means you can't do what you want. Why is it that you are not stressed? Somebody down the road in the same situation might be worried sick and not able to sleep.

HEADTEACHER: I'm in a situation that needs hassle and time to sort it out. I've taken what steps I can and the rest is not within my control. If I try to control what is not within my control I will stress myself and not function so well. I don't lose sleep over it because in time it will change, and if there is an even bigger problem, then I'll explain to the authorities how this came about. It doesn't keep me awake with worry because trying to change the balance sheet is a bit like trying to change the foreign exchange rate. If I have done what I can, then that's all I can do. The solution lies in knowing what you can control and what you can't. Emotionally, I may want to control things, but actually I can't, so there's no point in thinking that I can.

ME: But what do you say to someone who sees this deficit budget as a criticism of management ability and finds it hard to face colleagues? That can be a source of stress.

HEADTEACHER: It's nothing to do with the fact it's a budget. It's personality-driven. The headteacher down the road needs to keep up appearances more than I do, for her own security. I don't need that, but we're just different in what we need for our own security. Some headteachers need to space out things in their lives or are unhappy if events blow them about. I don't mind being in debt on my credit card. Other people might feel insecure about not paying everything off each month. Better to understand what you need to make you feel secure and live with it. If that's going to be perfectionism it's a pity, because there are ways to function without being a perfectionist. In knowing yourself better, you also have to look more carefully at the nature of the job and marry the two together. You may never do this until you are stressed and by then it's a bit late.

ME: But isn't the emotional level of stress too much to cope with to analyse things in the way you're suggesting? A person experiencing stress will say, 'I'm not coping. I can't keep on top of the job.'

HEADTEACHER: But what is the job? What is that you are conceiving as the job? People cannot change their personality, but they can change the way they conceive and define the job. It comes back to the fact that the job is undefined. If they are saying, 'I *should* be able to cope', then they have created an invalid or irrational definition of the job. It must be like that or they couldn't possibly see themselves failing. They will say, 'I'm not coping', but translated into real terms, what they are really saying is 'I'm not coping brilliantly at all times and in all circumstances'. The job is not to cope brilliantly, but to cope most of the time and fail occasionally. Once you get people to put aside unrealistic expectations you remove a lot of stress. Otherwise they will say to themselves, 'I must solve all problems perfectly in order to gain the approval of others and these problems must be dealt with quickly, preferably in the space of five minutes.'

Resistance to redefining the job comes by saying, 'But you're asking me to drop my standards.' This is irrational, because regarding the job differently is not the same as dropping standards. If redefining the job results in less stress and therefore functioning more effectively, standards could go up, not down. Peace of mind comes from saying, 'I've done what I can', or 'There's nothing more I can do about it'. Stress comes from still trying to control what is beyond control by putting in unnecessary effort to a lost cause. A perfectionist is no role model for a teacher to adopt who is already stressed. The targets set by a perfectionist are unrealistic for anyone else and, if truth be known, unrealistic for themselves. A more healthy position is to be realistic and ask what smaller target I can manage myself, not what target a perfectionist would seek. There are many ways to achieve high standards, not just one.

> When I think of the perfectionist on the staff, I know it does not stop with school. Her garden's tidy at home and her washing is folded. The cooker is clean and she's gone to bed exhausted if I telephone her in the evening. That's if she's not writing reports or planning for the following day. But that's how she feels good about herself. That's what makes her feel secure, so I live with it knowing that not everyone is going to be the same.
>
> (Headteacher)

If a second important message is 'know yourself', it is also a difficult one to implement. Working with my basic nature makes sense, but I may not know what that means or what my basic nature is. Am I able to deal with several things coming my way from all directions or do I need to take them one by one in a measured way? Do I need a great deal of approval and reassurance from people? Am I stubborn if I disagree with something? The need for approval in some teachers is very strong indeed, but energy-sapping. We all need recognition, but if we spend energy, thinking and emoting on demanding approval, even expecting approval we will feel worse if we do not get it (Rogers 1992: 6). The need for approval means we determine our worth by what people say, often mis-reading their comments as veiled praise or criticism when it is nothing of the kind. Approval from a colleague, headteacher or parent is uplifting, but hoping for it and expecting it are self-sabotaging states of mind. If we *expect* approval, we have said to ourselves, 'This person *should* recognise all the effort and skill I put into this.' There is no reason whatever why anyone should recognise anything because they may have more pressing thoughts about their own lives.

The examples I have used so far are about headteachers, who have some power and control over their lives. A source of stress for a main-scale teacher is to have to do something that the school, headteacher or government decided, with which they fundamentally disagree. The bottom line is that I am paid to do a job of work and at the moment it involves doing something I do not want to do. Initially I might be angry because I disagree with it and it is certainly going to be distasteful to do it. I can try to reduce the amount of 'myself' within it. If, for example, I have to test pupils for a government-inspired assessment that I believe is fundamentally flawed, what do I do? Suppose I feel very angry and manipulated. I can ask myself the following questions and provide some solutions.

Questions for analysis

Am I angry because this is something that makes everyone as angry as me, or do other people seem less angered?

If they are less angry than I am (and they *do* seem to be annoyed rather than angry), then it cannot be the assessment itself, can it? It must be something to do with the way I react.

If my anger comes from being totally opposed to it on ideological grounds, then how big an 'ism' is it? Is it a life or death 'ism'? Is it worth the emotional cost of protest, or can I find another way? Am I stubborn because of some irrational belief about status, pride or what other people think?

What are my solutions?

Solutions

If it is a big enough issue, I can refuse to do it and live with the consequences of that and its effect on colleagues who are prepared to assess this way. That might be unfair on them and could affect my future. If I really feel so strongly I will try to change things by coming up with something better. Result? A certain amount of stress and a lot of anger which is driving the stress.

If it is not worth the stress level and anger that go with resisting this, I will reluctantly do it.

A third example is about stress that is experienced because there are too many demands made on me at one and the same time. I might have a large number of children in a class and equipment not organised the way I would like. Some of it is missing and I cannot work in chaos. On top of this there might be too many pieces of work to mark and I want to do justice to all of them. The pupils, after all, deserve no less from me. Stress typically builds emotionally as three or more incidents or several ongoing commitments provoke a reaction. Added to this, the car breaks down on the way to school. A child in my class confronts me and disrupts the lesson I took so long preparing. Two pupils are teasing each other. If I'm a deputy headteacher, I might be faced by three irate parents in the space of an hour, and an upset teacher and caretaker in the next twenty minutes. A water pipe bursts and there is an unexpected visit from a fire safety officer. Stress like this is a bottleneck experience, but can focus the mind and emotions to the exclusion of everything else. Some of the stress in all these situations is generated through having to remain calm on the outside while possibly boiling on the inside. The worst combination of stressful reactions therefore becomes 'my day', and my day is characterised by a feeling that I cannot control my life, let alone the world or the Milky Way.

Analysis

There are at least eight demands and pressures on me. I feel inadequate because I believe I should be able to cope with these demands. If I can't, then I'm a bit of a failure in my own eyes. It threatens the way I want to be.

I'm used to being more in control. People even say how well organised I am. I can see my way through some of this, but the feeling sweeping over me is that I can't control what I want to.

Solutions

What's first? Nothing else matters because, stressful as it is dealing with eight things at once, I now have a queue. The reason why I get through is that I know the job comes at me in a variety of ways, and occasionally there is going to be a long queue. No question about that. I cannot see everyone at once or do everything at once. There will be a queue, and I can stop wasting emotional energy because I will inevitably inconvenience and disappoint somebody in order to please someone else.

What's first? If the room is disorganised and equipment missing, I cannot control that at the moment. Today we learn to share and cope. People, then equipment.

As one teacher said to me, 'The more out of control it is, the smaller the success needed to get it back on track.' As for paperwork, or the marking of too many pieces of written work, I have heard teachers say, 'I took time and trouble over the first six pupils and now I feel that the others deserve just the same.'

Analysis

I have run out of time because I did not define the boundaries of the job. I did the first six pieces of marking and now I'm burning the midnight oil to complete the rest.

If I do this because it will make me feel I have done justice to the paperwork and achieved something in the end.

If I do not do this, I will feel a totally rotten person who does not care.

Solutions

I can learn from this to define the job more realistically in future. It's nothing more than a queue or a bottleneck in the traffic.

I can mark four pieces of work a day until they are finished and disappoint some, but not all, pupils and parents about the time it takes.

I can burn the midnight oil and stress myself about what I am *not* doing instead of this.

A further solution is to try to change the way we self-talk this. We can talk up the problems or talk them down again. If we talk them up, we concentrate on all the things still to do, and they are *endless*. What will the mirror say on a bad day?

> I have marking to finish, lessons to prepare, a social services report to write and a reference. There is the plumber to contact and the dog to walk. The dishes are dirty and the washing is not done. And the house is like a rubbish tip. The lawn is as high as an elephant's eye and I have prepared nothing for tomorrow! It's parents' evening and my wall display is a shambles. The phone hasn't stopped ringing since I came home and now we've run out of bread.

What might the mirror say on a bad day?

> It just restores my faith in the Chaos Theory of Life. There are too many things pressing at the moment, so the reality is that all I can do is one of them.

In the classroom, my options are few when there is too much going on, especially when additional stress is triggered by the behaviour of a chronically disruptive pupil I will call Daniel. I cannot control Daniel's will and I cannot give him all my attention.

Solutions

I can say to the class, 'Daniel has had enough of my attention now and I need to teach all of you, not just one person, so we might need to ignore him.'

I can give Daniel time out or remove him and say, 'I'd like you to be involved in this, Daniel, but it's too expensive to teach you by yourself. So when you're ready to co-operate, you can join us because some of this is worth doing. Otherwise you'll have to do nothing, which is very boring.'

I can use a deflective statement to avoid confrontation and say, 'I can see you're angry . . . so we'll need to talk about this later.'

I can restate classroom rules: 'Daniel. You know the rule about stopping other people from working.'

I can state how I feel: 'I feel angry because I can't give my attention to other people who need it. I get very annoyed, Daniel, if I have to re-explain things.'

(Junior-school teacher)

I may have to tactically ignore Daniel unless he is verbally abusive, but even then, I can still have the remainder of the class on my side (Rogers 1992: 48). The change of viewpoint comes when I recognise this truth about life in classrooms:

> *I can control some things some of the time. I cannot control everything all the time, and that includes the behaviour of others. I can content myself with some control for some of the time and believe I am not a worthless or good person for doing so. There is no failure, only feedback and results, not mistakes. There are no errors, but there are chances to learn. Knowing this does not make it any easier.*

I have two final stress busters. A noticeable habit acquired through being a teacher is that, over time, we learn to scan the room while talking to pupils. A teacher will engage with a pupil, but try to be aware of what else is happening. This habit, alongside doing several things at once, tends to spill over into life outside school. Teachers can unfortunately become 'manic-vigilant' outside as well as inside school. Necessary though scanning is inside a classroom, there is a different experience to be had by not doing so elsewhere.

> Recently I met an old friend and supportive colleague. We both enjoy each other's company and I was visiting his workplace to examine assignments from a course he organises. He's witty and we bounce ideas off each other as we talk. As we chatted outside in the morning sun, I was aware of his habit of darting his eyes either side to greet other staff who were walking by. I have done the same myself many times before and maybe it's become a teacher's unfortunate trademark. Sometimes the mind is so full of other thoughts, it darts about and the eyes over-scan to left and right.
>
> But I know of another colleague who focuses on the person he is in conversation with and seems quite oblivious of anything else. Even in the briefest of encounters he is not distracted, but gives full attention and I feel quite different for that. A conversation with him is one which makes people feel valued. Giving full attention to a person is a quite different and positive experience not just for the recipient. The psychologist Dorothy Rowe (1988: 257) quotes a similar tale from one of her clients. 'I remind myself consciously that I'm going to make this experience with this person be of value, no matter whatever decisions could follow from it. This point in time is going to count, and that gives me freedom. I'm not so future-focused, thinking about my work and my contract. I'm in the room with the person, paying attention to what is going on.'

I can think of few better examples of learning to live in the moment. As one headteacher told me, however busy she is, if she wants to be less stressed she knows that it will happen through giving undivided attention. She used to do several things at once, apologise to visitors for interruptions, respond to the phone, search for documents and apologise again. But that only makes people feel as if they are in the way. All she succeeded in doing was making herself feel she was doing nothing properly. Now she probably gives as much time to staff, but it is more genuine when she focuses on the moment's experience. For her, the feedback she experiences is different.

My other stress-busting idea is about the stress experienced as a result of not understanding change, an area often outside anyone's control. Change may frequently be feared, but denying the reality of change has stressful consequences. The underlying unhealthy 'should not' driving the denial is 'Things *should not* change'. There is an allegory told as a story by Colin Thompson called *How to Live Forever* (1995: 26). In it a small boy searches the library for a lost book which has the secret of how to live forever. Night after night he searches until one night he meets four old men beneath a dusty shelf in the library attic. They are old, so cannot know about the book's secret, but take the boy through a Chinese garden to see an ancient child who is sitting on a tall chair. 'This young one has come for the book', the old man explains. 'You must not read it,' says the ancient child. 'It will drive you mad. I am the only person who has read it and not lost his mind. I was younger than you when I read it and I couldn't read it fast enough. Then, when my friends grew up I stayed like this. They grew out of toys and fell in love. They married and had children and all I could do was sit and watch. Now I am frozen in time. I kept saying that I had everything, but all I had was endless tomorrows. To live forever is not to live at all. That is why I hid the book.'

KEY POINTS

- Teaching is stressful because the job does not define itself. Therefore it is open to irrational definition.
- Irrational definition is most likely to lead to 'self-rating'.
- Teaching is a job that is always half-finished. If you can't set realistic boundaries, you'll live with stress. Get better at defining the job.
- There's no need to limit the job, but a great need to see realistic timescales and say 'No' when you have to. Stop trying to finish a job that is already defined as unfinishable.
- A key question about anything causing stress will be 'Is it within my control to do something?' If it is not possible to change anything, it may just have to run its course and I'll have to live with that.
- Stress comes from still trying to control what is beyond control. We can control some things for some of the time, but not everything for all of the time.
- A perfectionist is no role model for a teacher who is stressed.

- A Grade 1 as a teacher is a fiction undermined by the reality of having a good, bad, easy, difficult, rewarding and unrewarding week.
- When reality refuses to meet our demands what happens? We blame reality. Blaming prevents us from taking action to reduce stress.

Chapter 9

Positive teaching for the future

I began this book by writing about Sophie, whose label of special needs had fortunately been lost. I remain realistic rather than idealistic about pupils' abilities, but slightly suspicious when I hear generalised labelling of low ability and persistent unwillingness to co-operate. It is probably true for that teacher and that pupil at that particular time, but changes and surprises are possible. Positive teaching and learning are not about miracles happening, but about ways to trigger small but significant improvements. We can easily misjudge expectations, as this description of UK tests in English at Key Stage 2 (SATs) shows.

> When it came to the crunch in the SATs tests this year, the two laziest pupils wrote as if their lives depended on it. Most of the time, they do the very minimum to get by and these results just surprise me. I feel a bit duped now by their usual classroom behaviour, as if I've somehow been cheated by them all year. I had them down as low achievers, but actually they're nothing of the kind. There are some losses, because they had paid less attention all year of course, but they can do far more than I ever gave them credit for.
>
> (Middle-school teacher)

It will never be proved that this was asylum behaviour, where individuals behave much as they might be expected to behave in the circumstances in which they find themselves. Whatever the truth, the boys probably worked that year as pupils who were reluctantly compelled to do some work, rather than those who wanted to learn. There is no way of knowing this, but my experience has been that in most classrooms pupils develop remarkable skills in appearing to work, looking enthusiastic and tuning back into lessons just when they are needed. This is mainly why I have tried in this book to emphasise ways to ensure pupils are involved and accountable. I take the view that it is better to assume that pupils can achieve far more than, in my best judgement, I believe they can.

No teacher can persuade every pupil that it is worth the effort to learn, though the ability to motivate children comes high on any list of desirable teaching qualities. A snapshot picture of the classroom might reveal that these two boys are amiable, though they will achieve little in the time they have during a lesson.

They cause no serious trouble and produce the minimum needed to get by. Another two are going to take up valuable time because they will disrupt and entertain themselves and their classmates. They will do this instead of co-operating in learning because it suits them or they have another agenda. Other pupils will variously grind away writing, silently co-operate, have a great deal to say, be genuinely enthusiastic, rewarding to teach, resigned to their fate, upset, proud of themselves, elated or disappointed. As with their teachers, their interest, boredom, sense of achievement and disappointment will fluctuate.

Fortunately, the classroom is a place of shared values and concerns, so different responses and levels of ability are an accepted part of the orderly confusion. Teachers generally do the best that they can to take account of differences in ability and personality in their classrooms. They cannot possibly take account of all differences for all of the time, but can take account of some differences for some of the time. If I had to put hand on heart and reiterate the one feature of classrooms that most improves teaching and learning, it is the way in which feedback is given and used. Like the air we breathe, we can take feedback for granted because it is bound to be there in one form or another. In classrooms it ranges from a simple verbal exchange or feedback from a task to several pages of written response. Feedback is a passport to greater accuracy than wild guesses about what is happening. I have already made links in other chapters between feedback and self-talk, self-assessment and a teacher's language of descriptive praise. Some of the simplest skills in giving feedback can prove to be the most useful as a means of illuminating learning. Just because they are simple, it does not mean they are naive or that we already practise them.

> Martin, a trainee-teacher, was teaching year 6 children about mathematical ratios and had several practical examples, such as the size of books in relation to the surface of a desk. There came one of those moments I have seen so many times when a pupil is trying to answer a maths question, gets part way, then worries that the answer will be wrong. Sometimes you can see the worry on the child's face as a further question is asked when they're already under pressure. Usually this is a moment for an awkward pause and offers from other pupils after a prolonged silence, not always an opportunity for feedback to the pupil trying to answer. Martin, sensing this awkwardness, quickly intervened to say, 'It's OK, Adrian, you're doing fine. I'm just pushing you for more, that's all. I'm just pushing you hard for an answer to this.' The pupil, who by now seemed to be sufficiently reassured, completed his answer accurately and looked pleased. The exchange was not world-shattering teaching, but supportive feedback of a very simple kind. The technique was a very simple one, which was to be very open about what was happening.
>
> (Classroom observation, 1998)

The point this illustrated for me is not that Martin was exceptionally skilful in doing this. The point is that he did it at the moment when reassurance was most needed.

From problem-sufferers to problem-solvers

The teaching profession is full of people who find it difficult not to give in to expressions of the negative aspects of their job. Teaching is bound to have its disappointments and requires resilience that is not always there. Pupils can also find it difficult to focus on the positive and a number of them learn to be psychologically 'helpless' as a defence against making an effort (Seligman 1995: 111). For some teachers, it is the negative things that dominate as they focus on the difficulties at the expense of other aspects of teaching. Occasionally, teachers find themselves in a school where the ethos is predominantly negative, or where one or two members of staff generate a great deal of complaining conversation that is impossible to avoid. For many teachers, a negative focus is an unfortunate phase of difficulty.

> If you are going through a difficult phase with a class it becomes increasingly difficult to remain positive. If you are the least bit down, then the job is full of opportunities to be negative and see negative things. There is always something negative to be found in education, especially with demands for accountability weighing down heavily. You want to be positive, but it is so hard to find the energy sometimes.
>
> (Teacher in her first post)

If the time during which this happens is brief, it is probably manageable provided that a teacher recognises it as a bottleneck, and a temporary constraint. A much greater difficulty is that of dealing with frequent and pervasive negative conversation from colleagues or pupils. I described the way negativity feeds on itself in Chapter 1. Some pupils and staff can almost be relied on to be negative whatever the weather and see only difficulties and problems. Moans and complaints are of course justified in education. An allowable first flush of anger is usual as yet another government demand or staff frustration hits the desk, but what of a teaching or learning pattern which becomes 'draining', 'complaining', 'moaning' and 'negative' to the point where a member of staff is very difficult to live with. It is easy to get hooked into the way negative people get through their day. Bramson (1981: 48) explains that unjustified complainers and moaners in the workplace are rarely aware of the draining effect they have:

> Complainers do not feel they are whining. Their complaining is a doomed effort to warn about anything gone wrong that *someone else must fix*. Complainers persist in their complaining in order to validate their feelings that they themselves are not responsible. They are not responsible for doing anything differently or seeing things in a different way . . . while complainers do get attention, they rarely get action.

There are very good reasons why the sharing of gripes, moans and personal wounds is rewarding for anyone. Myss (1998) gives an explanation that I find particularly convincing. She explains that gripe-sharing between colleagues is a form of social intimacy, a way of developing or affirming trust. Two people can moan, complain and generally share wounds as a way of bonding, a process that works well so long as both parties tacitly agree to it. In the day-to-day contact in staffrooms and classrooms, some of this sharing of wounds and difficulties is necessary in order to validate feelings of frustration. The intimacy of moan-bonding helps to establish common, albeit negative ground. The more debilitating effects of negativity are likely to arise when individuals need to remain wounded and continue to share their wounds with a reluctant listener (Myss 1998: 14). This is no longer moan-bonding. Negative, critical and complaining conversation ceases to be shared feeling and becomes very draining. The source of energy is usually short-lived because people who are 'suppliers' soon realise that being around them makes colleagues feel that their energy is being drained. 'Drainers' are not 'moan-bonders' and have created predictable expectations about their griping. The negative unloading of problems inevitably reminisces impotently on the past, rather than looks forwards to the future. The perception for the moaner is often that of several events and circumstances contributing to the present dire situation. They may actually have done so, but the prevailing focus on 'reasons to feel aggrieved' is the very perception that is a barrier to a more positive outlook.

Moaners in the workplace can create frustration, fatigue and dull annoyance after a long bout of their griping. The more significant feature of Bramson's analysis for me is the idea that these complainers actually need to validate their feelings of not being responsible. He goes on to explain that moaning and complaining is often the only active behaviour that seems possible to those who feel powerless to determine their own fate. It is as if the complainers behave like powerless victims of imagined unjust forces that surround them. They may even have learned to do this as a social style resulting from any one of a number of reasons to feel thwarted. Even when things are going their way, they may still be pessimistically on the lookout for their falling apart. Bramson's view is echoed elsewhere. Markham (1993), for example, describes complainers and moaners as people who are not only draining, but who also have a strong need to decide to be negative in advance, thus protecting themselves from future disappointment. Markham describes a complainer as someone who, having complained, believes that they have done their bit and therefore need do no more.

From Markham's and Bramson's viewpoints, there is therefore a considerable hurdle to be overcome beyond acceptable moan-bonding:

• Negative griping provides a personal short-term gain, but can prevent solutions and may in time alienate colleagues.

- Positive responses from a colleague may ignore an individual's need to have their negative feelings validated.

This is a rather polarised position, and there may be a compromise involving acknowledgement of negative frustrations, accompanied by a shift towards problem-solving. Markham (1993) and Bramson (1981) have a similar solution to dealing with the problem of being sucked into the negative exchanges of problem-sufferers. Both these writers recommend briefly acknowledging to complainers that they feel as they do, but never agreeing with them that they are right. Acknowledgement of negative feelings is a necessary prelude to problem-solving. A technique favoured by Bramson is to use a descriptive statement which appears to clarify without judging, such as 'You're saying that my plans are too late to make any difference now. Is that right?' Another statement that acknowledges is 'Let's see if I understand what you're saying to me.' These non-judgemental summaries of the other's position contrast with statements which unwittingly agree, such as 'I'm sure I didn't mean it to sound like that' or 'We've got way behind with these plans. I'll admit it.' The attempt to agree, accepting responsibility, rather than simply acknowledging frustration simply lets the complainer off the hook. We have accepted responsibility, maybe even politely apologised, which gives the problem-sufferer an excuse not to do anything (Bramson 1981: 56). Blame has been fixed without regard to the complexities of a problem.

Like Felix the cat, we can go round and round in self-sabotaging circles if problem-suffering (reminiscing) becomes more attractive than problem-solving (searching for solutions).

> I've used this approach with a trainee teacher who blamed her dog, the sick children, a computer malfunction and her mother's illness for a variety of unfinished assignments. She reminisced about the fact that the car had broken down, the plumber was needed and the school that she was working in had the most difficult children in the country. She had lost files on the computer and her printer hadn't worked properly. She couldn't afford the repairs because she needed to pay the plumber. After what seemed a reasonable period of acknowledgement, and a great deal of attentive listening, I simply said, 'I think you need to move now from being a problem-sufferer to a problem-solver.' There was an understandably shocked silence as her future outfaced her past. But the time had come to kick-start problem-solving because we were getting nowhere.
>
> (Lecturer of Education)

Problem-solvers are individuals who have learned that it is usual to fail, feel bad and repeatedly try again until success occurs (Seligman 1995: 44). A teacher might encourage this by saying to a pupil, 'I want to hear what you have to say, then work with you to sort things out.' This strategy is really a deal that says that the pupil can let off steam and complain, so long as we both agree this will lead somewhere. The approach also avoids blame and implies action instead.

In summary, this approach has three stages:

- listening to pupil/staff moans until they are exhausted (difficult to do, but may be necessary at first);
- acknowledging the moaner, but never agreeing that they are right (much more effective and possible to do with practice);
- curtailing problem-suffering by directly asking for a shift to problem-solving (effective after acknowledging the moaner).

Bramson adds one further piece of advice when trying to move to problem-solving with a complainer. Complainers love to hook listeners into defending themselves, so they will accuse as they complain: 'There are not enough text books!' The defensive reply might be to say, 'Well, there certainly used to be', and follow this with a re-accusation such as 'If everybody [meaning you] looked after them, we wouldn't have a problem, would we?' Bramson points out that the pattern of *accusation*, *defence* and *re-accusation* escalates the problem-suffering and complaining. The re-accusation can be counted on to generate yet another defence and a further re-accusation, until an impasse is reached (Bramson 1981: 58). The accusation, defence and re-accusation pattern (ADR) confirms to both parties that blame lies elsewhere, usually with the other party. This, Bramson points out, makes it doubly important to describe and state the case without apology rather than reacting by defending or trying to prove it wrong. He also reassuringly says that the ADR pattern is most obvious with close friends and family members, because they have strong commitments to or expectations of each other. Maintaining politeness will hardly ever be a serious obstacle to accusing a very close family member of almost anything. Here, the pattern of ADR is at its heightened best. As I have reiterated elsewhere, knowing and understanding all this does not make it any easier. As a consolation prize, Bramson points out that we very often respond emotionally to events long before their exact nature has registered in our consciousness.

> I had a planning meeting with Di, the English co-ordinator, today, in which we both did some moan-bonding. She's not looking very happy this week, and I'm certainly not having a good time. We shared the frustrations of struggling to maintain high expectations and break through the apathy and resistance of these very difficult children. We did move on, though, to mirror each other's determination to keep at the task, and to find ways of reaching the children and encouraging them to engage more effectively with their work. We agreed that we had to accept their starting point, and work from there. It was an important conversation, for me anyway, because I NEEDED to share my frustration and fatigue with someone who understood. Because we both prefer to be positive about our job, we bolstered each other up. The

bonding moved the whole way through from moaning to reinforcing the positive.

(Middle-school teacher)

There is considerable stress in problem-suffering. Some of this stress can be explained by the way human beings adopt what Ellis (1998b) has polarised as sane and insane beliefs. A sane belief, he explains, is relatively free of stress, while an insane belief can be very stressful indeed, leading to feelings of hostility. Ellis would claim that it is perfectly sane to say to ourselves 'I don't like your behaviour' or 'I don't like this situation'. The stress-causing insane belief goes a stage further and says, 'Because I don't like your behaviour, you should not or ought not to display it.' A similarly stressful belief is to say, 'Because I do not like this situation, it should not be like this, or it *should never* happen.' The beliefs about 'should' and 'should not' lead to unproductive reminiscence about the past, blame of self or others, and unrealistic wishes for the future. Put much more simply, Bramson says, 'Stop wishing the difficult person or situation were already different.' The wish that someone were different is a magical wish, and even the greatest expenditure of energy will fail to make a change (Bramson 1981: 167). Even in the classroom where I might think that a pupil should not misbehave, the truth is that they did. I need them to behave differently (my need) and will take steps to persuade them (my plan), but I cannot actually control their will.

Some problem-suffering stress has its roots in unreasonable personal expectations of life and the things that 'should be' to make ourselves complete. Advertising is by no means an evil, but an example from therapist Carl Moog has given me pause for thought. On television programmes she often talks about insidiously created life expectations. She found, for example, that one of her depressed clients felt she was no longer living up to the 'Pepsi-Cola generation' of her youth. Time and again, there were references to advertising, how she 'should' have been and 'should' become, what she 'should' do and 'should' wear. She had internalised images, and integrated them into a set of expectations about who she was supposed to be. Failure to be socially adept and a happy member of a vibrant and successful generation had benchmarked her as a failed person. This was a pattern to emerge from a number of disappointed and disaffected clients. The advertisers had done their job very well, convincing the Sophies of this world that they should be part of a generation that looked, acted and drank in a specific way, achieved and were poised for success. Either they rated against the persuasive image, or they were excluded. This has been the case for a long time in successful advertising, and may well have raised unrealistic expectations where more realistic ones would do. The majority of the population is not over-influenced by advertising, depressed and disaffected, but persuasion and its consequent effect on self-raters can be very professionally done.

Feedback for the future

I concentrated in earlier chapters on the need for feedback to improve learning. When I think of receiving feedback myself, I do not rush to embrace it, probably for the same reasons as many other teachers. Feedback can be threatening as well as supportive, especially if it is taken personally. Feedback intended to improve learning is not naturally going to be perceived as positive by pupils or teachers unless we make it so. Although the backwash from formative assessment is usually positive, it needs to be seen that way by pupils if they are to cope with it. Improvement through feedback inevitably implies in some individuals' minds that something is less good than it could be and needs putting right. Formative feedback is also difficult for teachers to use because it involves analysis of learning, proposals for improvement and communication of a specific kind between teacher and learner. No wonder there is such a dearth of it. In order to keep track of every pupil's next stage in learning, a teacher would need to spend most of their evening reflecting on the day's teaching. While some teachers claim they do exactly this, it is unrealistic to expect it.

What is realistically possible? There are complementary strands to positive teaching and learning, not all of which are in the realms of fantasy or blind idealism. Suppose that the teacher became better informed, less stressed by events, and better at giving effective feedback to pupils about their learning. Suppose that pupils learned to be more self-aware and responsible, tenacious and self-rewarded if the feedback they experienced encouraged this. For this to happen, pupils would certainly need to be involved in giving feedback, but in a greatly enhanced way. It is easy to fall into the trap of thinking that the way to involve pupils is for the teacher to ask them plenty of questions. Quite the reverse has been demonstrated in a study of two outstandingly successful science teachers. They managed to teach in such a way that pupils asked over 60 per cent of questions (Garnett and Tobin 1989). Not surprisingly, the pupils were taught to do so. Creating such a classroom culture of inquiry is certainly possible.

I have found six aspects of teaching and learning relevant to becoming positive. The first concerns self-assessment as a means of becoming better informed about pupil progress. Self-assessment can encourage reflection, which then informs future teaching and learning (Chapter 5). Whatever the existing means of feedback, there is usually room for intensifying it through formative assessment, even if this is through rapid verbal feedback. The question is whether the effort needed to do this is worth it. I believe that it is, because a teacher who frequently gathers data on progress is far more in touch with what is happening. This of course assumes that the teaching style is one where pupils are active in delivering feedback. It also assumes that feedback is concerned with far more than whether or not pupils have completed a task. An additional reason for intensifying self and peer assessment is that it can help children take responsibility for their learning (Black and Wiliam 1998: 26). Pupils may become more self-aware through the feedback from their assessments. They stand a better chance of understanding what the teacher is trying to achieve.

Second, there are ways in which both pupils and teachers can avoid unnecessary stress through taking a more realistic, yet positive view of their lives. This includes learning to reframe negative responses to events, but mainly focuses on learning not to rate ourselves, but our performance instead, at that time. It is not too difficult to understand the workings of the proverb 'Pride comes before a fall'. If we rate ourselves as exceptional, instead of our enjoying our performance as being exhilarating on that day, at that time and in that moment, then we have set ourselves up for a fall. We rated ourselves. We took what was a moment of success and allowed it to stick to us as a more permanent rating. The ensuing difficulty is that any significant lapse in this high rating of self-worth is soon stressfully experienced as failure. Even if we have enormous talents and abilities, if we rate ourselves highly we have to display these abilities virtually all the time, just to maintain this fiction. Any lapse can lead to self-downing because we predefined what we call the 'high standards' necessary to support pride. Similarly, by rating ourselves because we did something badly on that day at that time, we damage our self-esteem. While success is desirable, it is not inevitable that insufficient success automatically equates with failure. Both 'success' and 'failure' are ambiguous, global and infinitely definable terms.

The third strand of positive teaching and learning concerns high expectations of there being feedback. Feedback expectancy is one of the most elusive qualities to be found in a classroom because it may be tacitly understood and generated through habit. We can check for its existence by asking:

- Do pupils expect that whatever the task there is a strong chance they will need to give feedback?
- Will feedback be demanded early in a session or project?
- Is feedback likely to be important?
- Is feedback the result of deadlines that have been set?
- Is there habitual discussion of feedback?
- Does feedback lead to further action?
- In short, is anyone going to check that I am working?

Feedback expectancy when well-established can drive learning forward without its being necessary to interrupt the flow of teaching. What matters is the ethos of accountability created, not whether feedback is actually given each time. So long as it is a frequent expectation, it will assist learning by keeping pupils involved.

A fourth strand of feedback is the use of descriptive praise. This, as I pointed out in Chapter 8, is a way of praising that allows pupils to credit themselves. In an ideal world, pupils would credit themselves out loud so that we knew what they had done. It is more likely they will credit themselves inside their heads, so we can only convey our pleasure by tone of voice when we describe. 'Brilliant' and 'fantastic' are not banned from my language, but the aim is not to use them in isolation from a great deal of description. I have no objection to enthusiastic adding of the words 'What do you think of that?' if I have a good feeling about the child crediting themselves. If I say something is 'fantastic' and add reasons why, I can feel justified with the descriptive additions. If pupils say 'fantastic' about their own efforts, that is much more rewarding for me to hear.

A fifth strand contributing to positive teaching and learning is one of developing pupils' positive self-awareness as a result of the feedback they encounter. This could easily be negative if teachers were unable to make classroom tasks sound possible and success seem achievable. The better side of self-awareness through feedback is a celebration of what is already achieved and a glance in the direction of what might be attempted. As teachers, we are there to support pupils' being and becoming. The driving force in all this is themselves, however accountable we may like them to be to us. We may inspire and interest them, but we cannot do more than hold a mirror to their capable and achieving selves. Far from abandoning responsibility as a teacher, one of the greatest tasks we have is to create the circumstances in which children can succeed. We have no need to accept poor work from them if we use feedback to spur them on to improvement.

The sixth strand is the harvest of my previous five. It is a harvest of hope, and entirely speculative. Pupils can learn to become responsible, tenacious and self-rewarded, particularly through descriptive self-praise and learning to reframe their worst perceptions. Some pupils naturally hang on in the face of difficulties despite the odds against them. In learning to become more tenacious, they will have learned to exchange problem-suffering for more positive currency. This is reciprocal, in that it poses challenging questions for teacher and pupils. Teachers may be adept at using descriptive praise with children, but are they able to describe their own efforts positively? Pupils may be on the receiving end of descriptive praise, but can they themselves learn to praise and feed this back to their teachers? Can teachers learn how to rate their performance, rather than rating themselves, and teach pupils to do the same?

If positive teaching and learning meant eradicating all our negative traits and personal weaknesses, we would be like see-through plate glass. There would be nothing left to reassure anyone that we were fallible human beings. There would be nothing left to reassure us that classrooms are imperfect places filled with the sounds of children. Where there is fallibility there is also creative tension, but where there is no fallibility recognised we lose credibility. The creative tension goes. We need creative tension because we are trying to think and learn, so creativity will always be needed to do that. Negative perceptions are worth disputing because they can so easily get in the way of problem-solving. The moan-bonding will of course go on as it always does, but so will the laughter of children. Beyond moan-bonding is confidence-provoking talk, reasonable and realistic positive description, as well as productive and useful beliefs in pupils' improvement. We may find that sustaining all this takes longer than we would like.

Bibliography

Abrams, M. and Ellis, A. (1994) Rational emotive behaviour therapy in the treatment of stress. *British Journal of Guidance and Counselling*, 22 (1): 39–50.

Andreas, B. (1996) *Strange Dreams: Collected Stories and Drawings*. Decora, IA: StoryPeople.

Babad, E.Y. (1980) Expectancy bias in scoring as a function of ability and ethnic labels. *Psychological Reports*, 46: 625–6.

Bandler, R. and Grinder, J. (1979) *Frogs into Princes*. Moab, UT: Real People Press.

—— (1982) *Re-framing: Neuro-linguistic Programming and the Transformation of Meaning*. Moab, UT: Real People Press.

Bennathan, M. and Boxall, M. (1996) *Effective Intervention in Primary Schools: Nurture Groups*. London: David Fulton Publishers.

Bennett, N., Desforges, C., Cockburn, A. and Wilkinson, B. (1984) *The Quality of Pupil Learning Experiences*. London: Lawrence Erlbaum Associates.

Bernard, M. (1986) *Staying Alive in an Irrational World: Albert Ellis and Rational-emotive Therapy*. South Melbourne, Australia: Carlson/Macmillan.

—— (1990) *Taking the Stress out of Teaching*. Melbourne: Collins Dove.

Bernard, M. and Joyce, M. (1984) *Rational Emotive Therapy with Children and Adolescents*. New York: J. Wiley & Sons.

Black, P. (1993) Formative and summative assessment by teachers. *Studies in Science Education*, 21: 49–97.

—— (1995) Can teachers use assessment to improve learning? *British Journal of Curriculum and Assessment*, 5 (2): 7–11.

Black, P. and Wiliam, D. (1998) Assessment and classroom learning. *Assessment in Education: Principles, Policy and Practice*, 5 (1): 7–75.

Blakey, M.L., Jahns, I.R. and Schroeder, W.L. (1971) The case of the self-fulfilling prophecy. *Adult Leadership*, 20 (6): 225–6.

Braiker, H.B. (1989) The power of self-talk. *Psychology Today*, 1: 23–7.

Bramson, R.M. (1981) *Coping with Difficult People*. Melbourne: The Business Library.

Brophy, J. and Good, T.L. (1986) Teacher behaviour and student achievement. In M.C. Wittrock (ed.) *Handbook of Research on Teaching*. 3rd edn, New York: Macmillan.

De Bono, E. (1991) The direct teaching of thinking in education and the CoRT Method. In S. Maclure and P. Davies (eds) *Learning to Think: Thinking to Learn*. Oxford: Pergamon Press.

Desforges, C.W. (1989) Understanding learning for teaching. *Westminster Studies in Education*, 12 (1): 17–29.

—— (1993) Children's learning: has it improved? *Education 3–13* (October): 3–10.

Doyle, W. (1986) Classroom organization and management. In M.C. Wittrock (ed.) *Handbook of Research on Teaching*. 3rd edn, New York: Macmillan.

—— (1990) Classroom knowledge as a foundation for teaching. *Teachers College Record*, 91 (3): 347–60.

Dreikurs, R. and Cassel, P. (1972) *Discipline without Tears*. Ontario: Alfred Adler Institute.

Dreikurs, R., Grunwald, B.B. and Pepper, F.C. (1982) *Maintaining Sanity in the Classroom*. London: Harper & Row.

Dryden, W. (1996) *Inquiries in Rational Emotive Behaviour Therapy*. London: Sage Publications.

Dweck, C.S. (1986) Motivational processes affecting learning. *American Psychologist* (Special issue: *Psychological Science and Education*), 41: 1040–8.

Ellis, A. (1962) *Reason and Emotion in Psychotherapy*. The Institute for Rational Living; 1991 edn, New York: First Carol Publishing.

—— (1975) *A New Guide to Rational Living*. Hollywood, CA: Melvin Powers Wilshire Book Co.

—— (1977) The basic clinical theory of rational-emotive therapy. In A. Ellis and R. Greiger (eds) *Handbook of Rational-emotive Therapy*. New York: Springer Publishing Co.

—— (1994) *Reason and Emotion in Psychotherapy*. Revised and expanded edn. New York: Birch Lane Press.

—— (1997a) Ask Ellis. Internet web page: Albert Ellis Institute (15 December).

—— (1997b) Achieving self-actualization. REBT featured Essay of the Month. Internet web page: Albert Ellis Institute (15 November).

—— (1998a) RET abolishes most of the human ego. REBT featured Essay of the Month. Internet web page: Albert Ellis Institute (15 April).

—— (1998b) Rational emotive psychotherapy. REBT featured Essay of the Month. Internet web page: Albert Ellis Institute (15 May).

Faber, A. and Mazlish, E. (1980) *How to Talk so Kids will Listen and Listen so Kids will Talk*. New York: Avon Books.

—— (1995) *How to Talk so Kids can Learn*. New York: Rawson Associates.

Garnett, P.J. and Tobin, K. (1989) Teaching for understanding: exemplary practice in high school chemistry. *Journal of Research in Science Teaching*. 26: 1–14.

Gillies, M. (1997) There's no success quite like failure. *The Guardian*, Management (8 November).

Gipps, C. and Murphy, P. (1994) *A Fair Test? Assessment, Achievement and Equity*. Buckingham: Open University Press.

Gray, J. (1992) *Men are from Mars, Women are from Venus*. New York: HarperCollins Publishers.

Howie, D.D. (1997) *NLP: Advanced Psychological Skills for the Thinking Manager*. Leighton Buzzard, Beds: Rushmere Wynne.

Humphreys, T. (1993) *Self-esteem: The Key to Your Child's Education*. Dublin: Gill & Macmillan.

—— (1995) *A Different Kind of Teacher*. London: Cassell.

—— (1996) *The Power of Negative Thinking*. Dublin: Gill & Macmillan.

Lidz, C.S. (1991) *Practitioner's Guide to Dynamic Assessment*. New York: Guilford Press.

Lindenfield, G. (1995) *Self-esteem*. London: Thorsons.

Lipman, M. (1991) *Thinking in Education*. Cambridge: Cambridge University Press.

McKay, M. and Fanning, P. (1992) *Self-esteem*. Oakland, CA: New Harbinger Publications.

McWilliams, John-Roger and McWilliams, Peter (1991) *You Can't Afford the Luxury of a Negative Thought*. London: Thorsons.

Markham, U. (1993) *How to Deal with Difficult People*. London: Thorson's.

Maultsby, M.C., Jr (1977) Basic principles of intensive rational behavior therapy: theories, goals, techniques and advantages. In J.L. Wolfe and E. Brand (eds) *Twenty Years of Rational Therapy*. New York: Institute for Rational Living.

Mills, D. (1997) Overcoming 'self-esteem': why our compulsive drive for self-esteem is anxiety-provoking, socially inhibiting and self-sabotaging. Internet web page: Albert Ellis Institute featured essay (November).

Mueller, C. and Dweck, C. (1998) Praise for intelligence can undermine children's motivation and performance. *Journal of Personality and Social Psychology*, 75 (1): 33–52.

Myss, C. (1998) *Why People Don't Heal and How They Can*. London: Bantam Books.

Nolen-Hoeksema, S., Girgus, J. and Seligman, M. (1986) Learned helplessness in children: a longitudinal study of depression. *Journal of Personality and Social Psychology*, 51: 435–42.

O'Connor, M. (1998) The power of feedback, *The Times Educational Supplement* (6 February).

Orbach, S. (1997) Too good to be happy. *The Guardian*, 'Weekend' (24 May).

Paul, R. (1987) *Critical Thinking Handbook: K3*. Rohnert Park, CA: Sonoma State University.

Rathbone, C. and Benedict, C. (1980) *A Study of Teacher Burnout at the Junior High School Level*. New England Teacher Corps Network, Portsmouth, NH. Sponsored by the Office for Education (DHEW), Washington, DC.

Rist, R.C. (1970) Student social class and teacher expectations: the self-fulfilling prophecy in ghetto education. *Harvard Educational Review*, 40: 411–51.

Rogers, W.A. (1992) *Managing Teacher Stress*. London: Pitman Publishing.

Rollinson, D. (1997) The disciplinary experience and its effects on subsequent behaviour. Paper for presentation at the BPS Psychology Conference (January).

Rosenthal, R. and Jacobson, L.F. (1968) Teacher expectations for the disadvantaged. *Scientific American*, 218 (4): 19–23.

Rowe, D. (1988) *The Successful Self*. London: HarperCollins Publishers.

Sadler, D.R. (1989) Formative assessment and the design of instructional systems. *Instructional Science*, 18 (2): 119–44.

Seaver, W.B. (1973) Effects of naturally induced teacher expectancies. *Journal of Personality and Social Psychology*, 28: 333–42.

Seligman, M.E.P. (1990) *Learned Optimism*. New York: Pocket Books, Simon & Schuster.

—— (1995) *The Optimistic Child*. New York: Houghton Mifflin Co.

Solomon, R. (1992) *Full Esteem Ahead*. Newport Beach, CA: Kincaid House Publishing.

Thompson, C. (1995) *How to Live Forever*. London: Random House Children's Books.

Tuckman, B.W. (1990) Group-versus goal-setting effects on self-regulated performance of students differing in self-efficacy. *Journal of Experimental Education*, 58 (4): 291–8.

Index